$100,000 per Year as a Freelance Writer: It's Possible, and Here's How

by

Jeff Rohde

J. Scott Digital

Copyright 2023 by Jeff Rohde/J. Scott Digital

All rights reserved

www.JScottDigital.com[1]

Cover photo by Sarah Dorweiler[2] on Unsplash[3]

---

1. http://www.JScottDigital.com
2. https://unsplash.com/@sarahdorweiler?utm_source=unsplash&utm_medium=referral&utm_content=creditCopyText
3. https://unsplash.com/photos/QeVmJxZOv3k?utm_source=unsplash&utm_medium=referral&utm_content=creditCopyText

Table of Contents

Who Are You? 1

Chapter 1 The Perks of Being a Freelance Writer 2

Chapter 2 From 9 to 5 to Six Figures: How To Transition From Your Day Job Into a High-Paying Freelance Writing Career 13

Chapter 3 Choosing Your Perfect Writing Niche 35

Chapter 4 Why Work for Cheap? How To Find Clients Who Are Willing To Pay What You're Worth 58

Chapter 5 Landing Your First Writing Gig: 10 Steps for Beginners ... 72

Chapter 6 Should You Work With an Agency or Go Directly to the Client? 90

Chapter 7 How To Find High-Paying Writing Jobs and Clients 98

Chapter 8 Fighting Lowball Offers and Negotiating Better Rates for Your Writing 112

Chapter 9 Tips for Keeping Your Clients Begging for More 125

Chapter 10 Simple Mindset Shifts To Help You Handle Rejection and Criticism 138

Chapter 11 Time Management Strategies for Freelance Writers 148

Chapter 12 Growing Your Freelance Writing Business 163

Chapter 13 You're Not Superhuman: How to Maintain a Healthy Work/Life Balance 179

Chapter 14 Diversifying Your Income: Why It's Important and How to Do It 192

Chapter 15 Why Freelance Writers Need Systems to Earn a Six-Figure Income 205

Conclusion Secrets of the $100,000 Club: Joining the Elite Rank of High-Earning Writers 232

About the Author 234

Who Are You?

Glad you asked. I'm Jeff Rohde, and welcome to my world of successful freelance writing. With over 25 years of experience in the business world, I've mastered the craft of copywriting and content creation, making it possible for me to earn six figures per year. I've written this book, "$100,000 per Year as a Freelance Writer: It's Possible, and Here's How," to help aspiring writers quit their day jobs and work as full-time freelance writers.

In my book, I share practical lessons I've learned as a freelance copywriter, including strategies for finding clients, negotiating rates, and creating captivating content that keeps readers coming back for more. While my experience is in real estate, finance and investment, insurance, accounting, and other business sectors, the strategies and techniques I've employed apply to all types of writers no matter their niche.

Through this book, I offer a blueprint for writers looking to transform their writing passion into a successful freelance career. From managing the business side of freelance writing to maintaining client relationships, my book covers all the key aspects of being a successful freelance writer.

So if you're ready to take the leap into the world of freelance writing, my book is an essential tool for achieving success. Get ready to learn how to quit your day job and earn a comfortable income working as a freelance writer - your dream is possible, and I'm here to show you how!

Chapter 1 The Perks of Being a Freelance Writer

Being a freelance writer is one of the most rewarding and liberating careers you can pursue. Not only does it give you unparalleled flexibility and control in your daily life, but it's also incredibly lucrative.

For starters, earning six figures (or more) annually as a freelance copywriter is possible. With no boss to answer to or salary cap, you can grow your income as much as you want by increasing your rates or taking on extra projects. You'll also enjoy tax benefits full-time employees cannot access, such as writing off business expenses like software subscriptions and office supplies or setting up a SEP IRA.

But money isn't everything – there are plenty of other perks too. As a freelance copywriter, you get to work on projects that interest you and reflect your unique skills and passions. You'll also be free to set your schedule – no more being stuck in an office from 9-5 every day of the week! Plus, you can work from anywhere worldwide without worrying about time zones or commutes.

As a freelance content creator, the world is your playground. With nothing but a laptop and a reliable internet connection, you can work from anywhere in the world. So, where are the best places to live the digital nomad lifestyle?

If you're looking for a popular destination, it's hard to beat Chiang Mai, Thailand. Chiang Mai offers low cost of living, excellent internet, and a vibrant community of digital nomads. Bali, Indonesia, is another popular spot with tropical beaches, lush greenery, and a relaxed lifestyle that's perfect for freelancers.

For those looking for something a bit more off-the-beaten-path, consider Brasov, Romania. This charming city, nestled in the Carpathian Mountains, offers a low cost of living, beautiful scenery, and top-notch internet access. Another option is Playa del Carmen, Mexico, which boasts beautiful beaches, delicious food, and affordable housing options.

No matter where you choose to live as a digital nomad, the key is finding a place where you can be productive and happy. These locations are just a few examples of the many great places around the world that offer the freedom and flexibility of the digital nomad lifestyle.

Of course, while living the digital nomad lifestyle can be an incredible experience, it's not for everyone. Many freelance writers choose to stay closer to home, and that's perfectly acceptable.

Writing is a craft that requires dedication and focus, and sometimes being in a familiar environment can help with that. By staying home, you can establish a routine, create a comfortable workspace, and eliminate the distractions that come with the travel and adventure of the digital nomad lifestyle.

Furthermore, for those with families or loved ones, the digital nomad lifestyle can be a challenge, making staying at home an ideal choice. Freelance writing allows for flexible work schedules, making it possible to balance creative pursuits with family responsibilities or other obligations.

In short, the decision to stay home and practice your writing craft is just as valid as the choice to live the digital nomad lifestyle. The key is to find the lifestyle that suits your writing style, and make it work for you.

Finally, there's the fulfillment of doing what you love as a career. With freelance writing, you can use your creativity and ingenuity in meaningful ways – helping others build their businesses or telling stories that impact readers' lives. And thanks to the power of technology, it's easier than ever to connect with those who need quality content, allowing you to make a real difference in the world.

Unlocking the Power Within

The phrase "the power within" is often used to describe the ability we all have to tap into our inner strength, courage, and resilience. It refers to the drive and resourcefulness that resides within each of us, regardless of our circumstances.

For writers, this phrase can be especially applicable. Writing requires confidence in your craft and an unwavering commitment to it even in the face of self-doubt or discouragement. This power comes from within, and it's what helps writers push through any obstacles on their path to success.

In freelance writing, unlocking your personal power within is essential for success. This power can be found in numerous forms, including creative confidence, self-motivation, and sharp discipline. As a freelancer, having faith in your capabilities is paramount. It's important to recognize that you have what it takes to succeed as a freelance writer. Cultivating that belief and having faith in yourself will enable you to take risks and strive for success, even when faced with the most difficult hurdles.

One such writer is J.K. Rowling, the author of the Harry Potter series. In the late 1990s, when she began writing the first book in the series, she was a single mother on welfare, struggling to make ends meet. She had faced numerous rejections from publishers before Bloomsbury Publishing picked up her manuscript. Even then, they only printed 1,000 copies of the first book in the series.

However, despite these setbacks, Rowling never gave up on her writing. Through hard work, perseverance, and incredible talent, she transformed herself into one of the most successful and influential writers of our time. Her books have sold over 500 million copies worldwide, and she is the first billionaire author in history.

Rowling's story is a testament to the power of perseverance and determination. It shows that no matter how many setbacks you experience, you can always tap into the power within and achieve your goals.

Beyond this sense of belief in yourself, strong self-motivation is also key to unlocking this inner potential as a freelancer. It's important to stay organized and on top of deadlines to ensure that projects are completed efficiently and on time. That requires staying focused and motivated despite any temptations or distractions from daily life. Developing an effective routine will help keep you on track so you can make the most out of your efforts as a freelance writer.

Finally, having strong discipline will go a long way toward helping unlock your inner potential as a freelancer. This means investing significant time into developing skills such as research abilities, writing proficiency, and time-management practices—essentially honing your craft daily under new challenges and scenarios. Doing so will improve your work quality and give you more confidence in yourself, which is essential when taking on new projects or tasks as a freelance writer. With dedication and hard work, there's no limit to what individuals can achieve.

Working for Yourself Instead of Someone Else

Another benefit of becoming a freelance writer is that you get to be your own boss. No one tells you what to write, when to finish a project, or how much to charge for each piece. A freelancer has complete control over their working environment, meaning writers can decide exactly what type of content they want to produce and how much they should charge.

Being a freelance writer brings a sense of pride and accomplishment in knowing that your work is entirely for yourself. You can determine what projects you would like to work on and how much time to devote to any given assignment, allowing for complete freedom and flexibility in which jobs to take and when. This opens up a world of possibilities for exploring new subject matter and taking on interesting assignments.

In addition, working independently also allows writers to grow and develop their skills by participating in various forms of professional development to stay ahead of the game. Freelancers can attend workshops, webinars, and write courses and books while learning more about their craft – without pressure from bosses or colleagues. With ample resources available online, such as specialized blogs and podcasts discussing various topics related to freelance writing, freelancers have virtually no limit when it comes to advancing their careers into something greater than themselves.

Discovering New Career Opportunities

Freelance writing also provides greater access to new opportunities. By diversifying into different areas such as copywriting, ghostwriting, creating websites, marketing content and social media posts, freelance writers open themselves up to new possibilities that would otherwise not be available in traditional settings. The variety of projects ensures that no two days will ever look the same and keeps life interesting for freelancers.

One of the many advantages of working as a freelance writer is the variety of projects that come your way. Unlike traditional jobs that can become monotonous and repetitive, freelance writing provides the opportunity to work on a diverse range of projects, which keeps things interesting and engaging.

As a freelance writer, you could work on anything from website content to email marketing campaigns, blog posts, white papers, and social media posts, among other projects. This variety of work ensures that you never get bored and that you're constantly learning new things and expanding your skill set.

Additionally, working on different types of projects allows you to diversify your portfolio and build a reputation as a versatile and adaptable writer. You'll be able to showcase your work to potential clients, demonstrating your abilities across multiple formats and industries.

Another benefit of working on a variety of projects is that you can choose the types of projects that interest you most. This allows you to take on projects that align with your personal interests and passions, which can lead to a more fulfilling and enjoyable freelance career.

Beyond the creative aspects, freelance writing is an excellent way to gain valuable professional experience. Working on various projects for different clients allows freelancers to develop their communication skills and build stronger relationships with potential employers or collaborators. Additionally, by taking on assignments from many different companies, individuals can learn how businesses operate from the inside out and equip themselves with important market knowledge that will be invaluable in their future careers.

Furthermore, being part of the freelance writing community allows writers to engage with other creatives and grow their networks. From joining online forums to attending industry events and meetups, freelancers have access to an array of exclusive resources which can lead them down new paths according to their interests and goals. With so much diversity available at one's fingertips, it is no surprise that the number of digital nomads has dramatically increased over recent years.

According to a recent survey by MBO Partners, a business consulting firm, the number of independent workers in the United States alone is expected to reach 47.2 million by the end of this year. Many of these workers are digital nomads who work remotely while traveling the world.

Furthermore, a recent survey by Upwork, a leading freelance platform, found that 59 million Americans freelanced in 2020, an increase of two million from the previous year. The survey also found that the number of full-time freelancers increased from 7.7 million in 2019 to 9.2 million in 2020.

These figures demonstrate the increasing trend towards remote work and digital nomadism. As technology improves and people seek greater flexibility and autonomy in their work, it's likely that these numbers will continue to rise in the coming years.

Reinvesting in Your Business

In addition, freelance writing gives individuals greater financial autonomy by allowing them to set their own rates and have a steady income stream each month. As new clients come on board and assignments are completed quickly and efficiently, this can lead directly to increased earnings, which can then be reinvested into further business development, such as buying better software or building websites, or investing in alternative "passive" income streams.

Professional freelance writers can benefit from several different software applications designed to help increase their writing productivity and efficiency. For instance, many freelancers swear by tools such as Grammarly for spell-checking and automatic punctuation or Hemingway for writing guidance. Similarly, ProWritingAid (PWA) provides a more in-depth analysis of writing samples for those looking for more detailed feedback on their content.

Some other popular software applications include Google Docs for collaboration and cloud storage, Scrivener for organizing projects, Slack for communication purposes, Trello for efficient task management and Asana, which allows users to set specific goals and deadlines while tracking progress along the way.

When it comes to financial freedom, freelance writing can be a great way to take control of your finances and set yourself up for success. Depending on the type of writing assignments you choose, freelancers can often negotiate higher rates as their skillset grows, meaning they can earn even more than before. More experienced writers may also be able to diversify into niche markets that offer greater potential for higher earnings. These niche markets may be in the business-to-business (B2B) sector, business-to-consumer (B2C) sector, or within specific industries.

For example, B2B niches might include technical writing, medical writing, grant writing, or scientific writing. These areas require specialized knowledge and expertise, and writers with experience in these fields can demand higher rates for their work.

In the B2C sector, niche markets might include travel writing, food writing, or lifestyle writing. These areas may require a writer to have specific experience or expertise, such as experience traveling to exotic locations or knowledge of nutrition and food preparation.

Within specific industries, there are also numerous opportunities for niche writing. For example, a writer with experience in the real estate industry might specialize in writing content for real estate websites, creating social media posts for real estate agents, or composing marketing emails for real estate agencies.

A writer with experience in the legal industry might specialize in creating content for law firm websites or writing legal blogs for attorneys. A writer with experience in the financial services industry might specialize in writing newsletters for investment firms or creating content for financial websites.

The possibilities for niche writing are endless, and by diversifying into these niche markets, experienced writers can not only earn higher rates but also establish themselves as experts in their respective fields.

As a bonus, with digital tools on the rise, freelancers can increase productivity and reach new audiences quickly and easily. Many freelance writers have also created blogs or websites to showcase their expertise and generate additional income. Blogging enables a writer to share their work with a larger audience and potentially monetize their blog with advertising revenue or affiliate marketing. Websites, on the other hand, can be used to create an online portfolio of a writer's work, promote services, and gain exposure in the industry.

Blogs and websites can also be used by freelance writers to showcase their knowledge and experience in a particular field. For example, a writer specializing in travel might create a blog or website featuring destination guides, reviews of local businesses, and advice for travelers. A food writer might create a blog or website featuring recipes, health tips, and restaurant reviews.

Ultimately, when it comes to financial freedom, freelance writing provides many opportunities for growth and development that might otherwise be unavailable.

Leveraging Freelance Writing Platforms

Finally, while businesses often become stagnant after some time due to limited resources (time & money), freelance writing presents an exciting platform whereby opportunities are constantly being presented through platforms like Upwork or Fiverr–which enable even newer contractors starting out in the industry secure projects with ease thanks to platforms like these.

Upwork and Fiverr are two of the most popular platforms for freelance writers, offering freelancers the opportunity to find work more easily:

- Upwork offers access to a global network of clients with projects posted daily, allowing freelancers to search for jobs by keyword or category based on their individual skill sets and experience.
- Fiverr provides a unique system that enables new freelancers to showcase their talents and find creative projects that match their skills. It also allows users to apply for 'micro-tasks,' which can be completed quickly and efficiently, resulting in regular income.

Through both platforms, freelancers in competitive markets can create an effective portfolio of past accomplishments to show potential clients as proof of their expertise. This is a great way for freelancers to stand out from the crowd and demonstrate their abilities. By showcasing prior work samples, clients can get an idea of the quality of work they should expect when working with that specific writer.

Additionally, having a portfolio of past accomplishments will help establish credibility and trust with potential clients. They know that the freelancer they are considering has a proven track record and that they are unlikely to be disappointed with the work delivered.

Having an online portfolio also allows writers to display a wider selection of previous samples than what might normally be included on a resume. This gives writers more opportunities to showcase their talents and make an impression on potential clients. It also helps freelance writers stay competitive in markets where competition for projects is fierce. Ultimately, these platforms make it easier for freelance writers to succeed and earn the financial autonomy they desire.

All in all, numerous distinct advantages come with being a freelance writer:

- Freedom over working hours and style.
- Having control over projects and rates.
- Access to additional revenue streams.
- Improved financial autonomy.
- Freshness and creativity are enabled by engaging multiple audiences through innovative methods.

Just to name a few. In reality, the list really does go on and on.

Chapter 2 From 9 to 5 to Six Figures: How To Transition From Your Day Job Into a High-Paying Freelance Writing Career

As a full-time freelance writer, I often get asked how to make the transition from working 9 to 5 in a day job to pursuing a career as a high-paying freelancer. It can be challenging, but if you start small and set manageable goals for yourself, you'll find that the transition is achievable. To begin with, try to generate enough extra income on the side to replace one week's worth of gas or groceries. Once you reach this goal, aim higher and continue setting interim targets until you're earning enough to completely replace your salary from your day job.

In this chapter, we'll explore what it takes to become a successful freelancer - from setting up your business to having the right mindset and doing things differently than traditional employees. We'll cover topics related to the business of freelance writing, such as finding clients, setting up an effective workflow and managing income.

We'll also discuss how to develop a successful writer's mindset so you can tackle any challenges that may arise along your journey. Finally, we'll look at what sets successful freelance writers apart from their peers and how you can use these strategies to craft a successful career for yourself.

The Business of Freelance Writing

Transitioning from a regular 9-5 job to becoming an independent, high-paying freelance writer requires dedication and a clear vision. As with starting any business, many steps must be taken to ensure success.

There are many things you need to consider before taking on freelance writing, including:

- Assessing your skills and interests.
- Networking with other professionals.
- Starting small before fully jumping into freelance writing full time.
- Building your online presence.
- Budgeting for expenses.
- Researching potential clients.
- Keeping track of income and taxes.
- Finding mentors who can provide valuable insights.

Further still, one must do everything one can to attract high-paying clients who value their work and develop strategies to take calculated risks that can take their business to the next level. Let's look at some tips and tricks which will help navigate these waters so that anyone looking to make a transition can start their journey towards becoming a successful freelance writer:

1. Assess your skills and interests - what are you good at and passionate about? This will help guide your search for freelance opportunities.

Assessing your skills and interests is important when transitioning from a regular 9-5 job to becoming a freelance writer. Doing so will help you determine what type of freelance opportunities you should pursue. What kind of writing do you enjoy? Do you have a knack for creative writing, or are you more of an analytical writer? Are there certain topics that interest you, like business, finance or science? All of these elements should be carefully analyzed and considered when looking to become a freelance writer.

It is also essential to evaluate what you are passionate about and how this might fit into the world of freelance writing. Assessing your strengths and weaknesses can help guide future strategy decisions. For example, building relationships with clients needing content creation services would make sense if you excel at creative writing but aren't particularly interested in technical aspects such as SEO optimization. On the other hand, if research and fact-checking come naturally to you, honing those skills could lead to bigger breakouts.

Taking the time to assess yourself before diving into freelancing full-time puts you in a better position to make informed decisions about finding work, setting rates and managing your workload. This ultimately leads to greater success as a freelance writer since your skill set has been tailored specifically for your chosen niche and what potential clients may be seeking.

2. Network with colleagues and connections in the industry to find out about potential freelance opportunities.

Networking is key when it comes to making the transition from a full-time day job to becoming a freelance writer. Connecting with colleagues and others within the industry can be incredibly beneficial in helping you find potential freelance opportunities. Building strong relationships with influencers, potential clients, editors, writers, and anyone else with a hand in the industry will help build your network and grow your career.

By attending events, joining online forums and actively engaging with people on social media, you can establish yourself as someone knowledgeable in the field. Not only does this give you access to new contacts, but it also builds crucial relationships where you are more likely to hear about projects or tips that may have otherwise been missed out on. Additionally, getting informal advice from those already ingrained in the industry can provide invaluable guidance - something that cannot necessarily be found through research alone.

Network building doesn't stop once you've established a few key contacts; it should be an ongoing process as business trends shift and relationships evolve. As long as you remain active within circles relevant to your chosen freelancing field - whether it's staying up-to-date on the news, attending events or simply reaching out via email or direct messaging - there will always be new connections to make.

3. Start small, with side gigs or freelance projects during your free time, before fully transitioning to freelancing.

Making the transition from a full-time job to becoming a freelance writer isn't something that should be done impulsively. It can take time and patience to establish yourself in the industry and find worthwhile projects, meaning starting small is important. One way of doing this is by taking up side gigs or smaller freelance projects during your free time - this allows you to dip your toe into the freelancing world while still having the safety net of a steady income and building up your capital reserves.

With small projects, you can hone your skills and gain more experience in different writing styles or topics. Getting familiar with various industries will help broaden your portfolio, which could make it easier once you decide to go full-time as a freelancer. Additionally, side gigs or one-off projects are great for forming relationships with new clients and gaining referrals. This interaction is key when creating a strong network that will sustain you through future projects.

Starting small should not discourage you from jumping into freelancing full-time. Rather, it should provide an opportunity for growth and exploration before committing fully to this path. This way, if something doesn't turn out as expected, you still have other sources of income available until you have established yourself in the freelance industry.

4. Build a strong online presence with a solid portfolio and social media accounts dedicated to your freelance career.

Having a professional portfolio website showcasing your best work and outlining how you can help potential clients is the first step to taking your career to the next level. Additionally, having social media accounts dedicated to your freelance career helps you build a network with industry professionals and gives your work much-needed visibility.

When curating your portfolio, focusing on quality over quantity is important. A few select pieces that showcase your strengths as an expert in writing will be much more effective than an expansive list of every piece you've ever written. Similarly, creating accounts specifically for professional purposes on popular platforms such as Twitter and LinkedIn helps ensure that your shared content is relevant and of interest to potential employers or clients. Not to mention keeping your personal life separate from your working world.

However, it's not enough to create these social media profiles. Consistency is key to building a strong online presence for your freelancing career. Posting regularly with meaningful and targeted content allows others within the industry to become familiar with you and your services. This familiarity could go a long way in helping to land new opportunities or projects down the line.

5. Set aside money for startup expenses like equipment or marketing.

Equipment is an integral part of being a successful freelancer, so having enough money to purchase all necessary devices, such as a laptop or printer, will be invaluable as you progress in your chosen profession. Additionally, it's important to remember that some investments might not be tangible – marketing efforts are key when launching any business, freelance included. Having sufficient funds dedicated to using advertisements or websites is a great way to increase visibility and reach more potential clients.

It's also worth remembering that setting aside funds doesn't just apply when starting out. Throughout your freelancing career, it's essential to always have some resources saved up in case of unexpected expenses or a lull in projects. This cushion will ensure you're covered in an emergency and can help reduce any anxiety associated with taking on last-minute jobs for less-than-desirable clients.

6. Research possible clients and markets for your freelance services.

Speaking of clients, researching potential new accounts and markets is essential for building a successful freelance career. By taking the time to understand the needs of different industries, freelance writers can gain valuable insight into the particular types of services and solutions that are in demand. This helps them to create more targeted content that meets the needs of their clients. Additionally, by understanding the needs of a given industry, freelancers can better position themselves in terms of offering their services and tailor their offerings specifically for businesses and organizations within those industries.

In addition to positioning themselves well in terms of offering specific services and solutions, having a deeper understanding of an industry also gives writers greater insight into topics they can write about within that industry. As a result, they can create more meaningful content that adds value to their clientele and increases their chances of success with their projects. This research should also extend to understanding any possible legal requirements in the market for freelancing so that you are always aware of what is expected from you.

By studying various publications within your industry and talking with other professionals, you can get a good idea of who is seeking these types of services and pinpoint the best way to reach them. Additionally, researching competitor websites or social media accounts may provide valuable insights into how other freelancers are marketing themselves and introduce new strategies you can incorporate into your efforts.

It's also crucial to establish yourself as an expert in your field by investing some time in general knowledge surrounding the subject. Doing so will make it easier for potential clients to trust your abilities, as they will be more confident that you have the skills needed to complete their project effectively. By thoroughly researching possible clients and markets, you can ensure that your freelance career receives a strong start and continues thriving over time.

7. Keep track of contracts, invoices, expenses, and taxes as a self-employed individual.

This includes contracts, invoices, receipts for expenses, and even taxes. By maintaining accurate records of these items, you can ensure that all relevant information is readily available when needed. Having your contracts in order makes it easy to refer back to them in case of client disputes and allows you to easily document the services provided and payment terms. Additionally, tracking invoices helps you know when they are due while also offering an overview of the income generated by each job.

Also important is monitoring various tax payments throughout the year so that you don't end up owing a large sum come April 15th. It's best practice to pay estimated taxes quarterly to avoid underpayment penalties - this can be done through IRS direct debit or other payment plans set up with your state government.

8. Find a mentor or join a community of fellow freelancers for support and advice on building a successful career.

A mentor can provide personalized advice based on their own experiences while helping you plan your career goals. Additionally, having access to an experienced professional can help you navigate tricky situations and bridge any knowledge gaps to reach the next level.

While there is always a risk that mentoring a beginning writer could create more competition, the potential benefits to the mentor are greater. Mentoring helps experienced writers stay connected to their craft and renew their passion for writing. It also gives them the chance to share their knowledge with others, build relationships and gain insight into new ideas and approaches. Plus, it can give them the opportunity to establish themselves as an authority in their field and increase their professional credibility within the community. Ultimately, despite the risks of creating competition, mentors can benefit from taking on a mentee by strengthening existing skills and gaining valuable experience in teaching and leadership.

Being part of a community of freelancing peers can be equally beneficial as it offers the opportunity to collaborate, share ideas, and receive feedback from like-minded individuals. It's also an excellent way to connect with people who understand the day-to-day challenges of running your business and offer solutions when needed. Lastly, joining such a group can inspire you to stay motivated toward reaching success.

9. Continuously improve and expand your skill set to stay competitive in the industry and attract higher-paying clients.

In the ever-changing world of freelancing, improving and staying one step ahead of the competition is important. A great way to start is by researching industry trends and topics related to your area of expertise – this way you can stay up-to-date on the latest technologies and strategies available. You can also stay sharp by reading industry publications or attending seminars or workshops on your chosen craft.

It's also worth exploring areas outside your comfort zone, from graphic design to SEO or social media marketing. Having a diverse skillset expands the potential for new business opportunities and allows for more creative problem-solving. Not only will this help attract higher-paying clients, but it could lead to an entirely new career path. Also, don't forget to take advantage of any free online courses that may be available - these can be great resources for learning new skills while keeping costs low.

In addition to seeking outside support, staying proactive by dedicating time each day to writing exercises and improving your skillset is important. Writing daily will sharpen your craft and expand your understanding of various topics - this will come in handy when working with new clients or tackling challenging assignments. Continuously improve and expand to stay competitive in the industry and attract higher-paying clients – writing daily will definitely help.

10. Be willing to take risks and try new things to continue growing as a freelancer and reaching new levels of success in your career.

While being cautious and strategic when taking risks is important, pushing yourself outside your comfort zone can often lead to positive results. Whether that means learning a new skill, taking on a difficult project, or trying something out of the box – the effort could be worth the extra effort.

Calculated risk-taking can help maximize potential rewards while minimizing unnecessary losses. One great example would be diversifying your skill set. As mentioned above, exploring options outside your chosen specialization allows for more creative problem-solving and positions you for higher-paying projects. You could also try pitching to bigger clients or rebranding yourself to fit their needs - this type of risk-taking shows initiative and dedication, often leading to remarkable opportunities.

One notable example of a contemporary risk-taker who ultimately found success is Jessica Hische. After graduating from art school, she decided to take a big risk and become a freelance lettering artist, illustrator, and web designer. Despite the challenge of going out on her own without the security of a full-time job, Jessica persevered and was eventually able to establish herself as one of the most sought-after commercial lettering artists in the world. Her work has been featured in numerous magazine covers, advertisements, book covers, television shows, and music albums. She even wrote her own font library which is now available for free online. Through hard work and taking risks, Jessica was able to turn her passion into a successful freelance career.

Don't be afraid to experiment with different marketing or promotional tactics either - this could broaden your audience reach and ultimately bring in more business from potential clients worldwide. Lastly, consider investing money into relevant courses or certifications that can boost your expertise and help set you apart from other freelancers competing in the same space.

At the end of the day, being willing to take risks and try new things is one of the best ways to keep growing as a freelancer and reach higher levels of success in your career. By taking calculated risks such as expanding your skillset, pitching larger clients, experimenting with various marketing strategies, or investing in further education – you will be giving yourself sizable advantages while setting yourself up for long-term success.

The Mindset of a Successful Freelance Writer

Creating a successful freelance career is more than just having the necessary technical skills and a portfolio of quality work. It's also about having the right mindset to stay motivated and driven in this unique line of work. Having the proper motivation, drive and enthusiasm is key to creating a successful freelance career. When freelancers stay focused and hone in on their goals, they can look past short-term difficulties and reach success. A positive attitude helps freelancers tackle problems head-on, push through difficult times, and remain resilient during challenging situations.

Here are some qualities of a successful freelance writer:

- They possess a "growth mindset" – they understand that there will always be something new to learn and strive to keep their knowledge up-to-date. They are open-minded, willing to take risks and embrace change enthusiastically, knowing it can lead to exciting opportunities. They also know how to manage their time effectively, easily balancing workloads and personal commitments.

- Another important element for success is resilience – things might not always go as planned, and you will have to adapt quickly and make decisions on the fly without panicking. An attitude that embraces failure as part of the learning process can help you overcome setbacks faster.

- Success depends on being proactive - staying organized, setting clear goals, connecting with colleagues in your field of expertise, and researching potential opportunities. These are all key activities that need consistency if you're looking to reach higher levels of success. A successful freelancer must also possess superior communication skills - they should be able to explain complex topics in simple words while maintaining accuracy and understanding at all times.

- They know that success is often determined by effort rather than talent alone – doing what others won't do today makes it easier to achieve tomorrow's successes. Most importantly, the best freelancers recognize when to take a break from working or step away from projects that don't align with their personal or professional values. Knowing when to take a bit of time off is essential for mental health and overall success.

Creating a successful freelance career requires more than just great writing skills and an impressive portfolio – having an appropriate mindset is equally important to reach new heights in your profession. From developing a growth mindset and embracing change to exhibiting resilience during hiccups along the way– these traits can help any freelance writer succeed.

10 Things Successful Freelance Writers Do Differently

Successful freelance writers often have something that sets them apart from the rest. They take a proactive approach to their career and understand the importance of constantly investing in themselves, having the courage to say 'no' when necessary, and understanding the industry and market trends.

$100,000 PER YEAR AS A FREELANCE WRITER: IT'S POSSIBLE, AND HERE'S HOW

It's also essential that successful freelancers are always learning - staying up-to-date with industry news, exploring new tools, or mastering software can greatly improve your capabilities, adding more value for potential clients. Understanding market trends will also help you maximize rewards while negotiating fair payment rates. Don't be afraid to ask for what you believe you deserve.

Finally, strive to build an authentic personal brand that stands out from the competition. This could open even more doors as clients appreciate working with professionals who have a purpose behind their actions rather than just looking for quick payoffs.

One example of a contemporary writer and entrepreneur who has built a successful personal brand is Seth Godin. Over the years, he has successfully used digital marketing to promote his books, blogs, podcast and other creative work. He has also been involved in many entrepreneurial ventures such as Squidoo and Yoyodyne Entertainment.

Another example is Gary Vaynerchuk, an American entrepreneur, author and public speaker known for his success in social media marketing. Vaynerchuk built his personal brand through entrepreneurship and content creation including books, podcasts, web TV shows and YouTube videos. Lastly, there is Marie Forleo - another successful entrepreneur who uses her platform to help others achieve their goals through digital marketing strategies like email lists, blogs and social media campaigns.

These combined qualities can make a huge difference between success and failure as a freelance writer. Let's take a closer look at each:

1. Prioritize networking and building relationships with editors and clients.

As a freelancer, networking and building relationships with editors and clients is crucial for success. It's important to understand the needs of editors, from what kind of stories work best in their publication to where you can look for more assignments. Editors will appreciate your knowledge and professionalism and will be more likely to offer better opportunities if you demonstrate authenticity, enthusiasm, and meaningful connections.

When building relationships with clients, it's essential to focus on communication. This includes listening carefully to their needs, responding promptly and politely, and proactively offering solutions or ideas that might not have been discussed initially but make sense in context. A successful freelance writer should also show versatility by being willing to take on different types of tasks, whether creative content or technical write-ups. Showing your ability to adjust quickly depending on the situation will impress any client.

Freelancers should always aim high and strive for greatness, which shows dedication and passion for the job, which clients appreciate more than anything else. Making yourself available for questions or additional requests also indicates that you are invested in the project, which may lead to even more rewarding collaborations down the road.

2. Value consistent work ethic and productivity.

Consistent work ethic and productivity are key to a successful freelance career. A freelancer must stay motivated and driven to produce high-quality work regardless of the circumstances. If you're having trouble with motivation, break down your projects into smaller tasks to make progress towards larger goals. Always maintain professional standards by delivering on time and within budget.

Freelancers also need to be careful not to overload themselves. Too many assignments can lead to subpar results, so you must prioritize the most important tasks first. Create a schedule for yourself and stick to it as much as possible. Doing so will help you stay on track with deadlines and achieve more in less time, helping to maximize your billings for each hour spent working.

The ability to use resources effectively is also essential in any kind of job but especially when working independently as a freelancer, as this is often all you have at your disposal. Utilize technology such as time-tracking apps or project management tools which can be extremely beneficial in staying organized and efficient with your work. Also, consider connecting with other freelancers who may offer insight on balancing workloads while maintaining a healthy standard of quality work.

Finally, don't forget that taking breaks is just as important. Freelancers should be mindful of their physical and mental health while persevering through their projects. Regular pauses throughout the day will allow you stay mentally fresh, which can help boost creativity, focus, and productivity.

3. Know how to manage time effectively.

As a freelancer with numerous clients and different deadlines, managing your time efficiently can be the difference between success and failure. Setting realistic yet challenging goals for yourself is essential to stay on top of projects and remain productive. Make sure you have enough time to complete each task - do not allow yourself to be under pressure or accept more work than you can handle.

Creating a schedule for yourself can also help you stay organized and maximize your day. Don't over-schedule so you're constantly rushing from one task to another, resulting in lower-quality work. Leave adequate time for rest or leisure activities as well. Taking breaks or getting away from work for even a short amount of time can help reduce burnout and stress.

Staying focused on one task at a time is important too, as multitasking may lead to confusion and lost productivity. Identifying what tasks need your undivided attention first will enable you to finish more quickly while still producing high-quality results. Lastly, it's important to remember that no two days are alike - things come up unexpectedly, and some timelines may be shorter than others. So, always leave room within your schedule for these unplanned occurrences.

4. Constantly learning and improving.

As a freelance writer, it's essential to constantly work on learning and improving your writing skills. Staying up-to-date with the latest trends and techniques in the writing field will help you better serve your clients and understand their needs. Developing new skills such as copywriting, storytelling techniques, or editing can also open various opportunities you may not have known about before.

Staying motivated to learn is key - set goals for yourself each week, such as reading a blog post or practicing a specific skill. These practices will keep you engaged even if the tasks are smaller in scale. Additionally, seek feedback from people who can provide helpful critiques that may identify improvement areas or ideas for advancement.

Remembering that learning doesn't end with technical skills is also important. Keeping track of industry trends, understanding what sells and developing persuasive vocabularies are all valuable assets for any freelance writer. It takes dedication to stay sharp, so don't be afraid to take risks and push yourself further - experimentation often leads to creative breakthroughs.

5. Have a strong understanding of the industry and market trends.

It's essential to stay up-to-date with the latest writing styles, topics and formats, as these can vary from client to client. Understanding what is selling in the current market will help you create content that resonates with clients and readers.

It's also important to watch industry news to recognize changes or emerging trends that could influence your work. Reading the works of successful authors and attending workshops to enhance your skillset are great ways to stay informed. Additionally, seeking out feedback from experienced professionals can be invaluable in keeping you up-to-date on best practices and industry standards.

Developing a strong market awareness will also enable you to better serve your clients' needs by offering creative solutions and insights that may not have been considered earlier. For example, a web developer might keep an eye on the latest UX design trends from niche industries and use this information to create unique designs for clients in those industries. Similarly, a copywriter could track SEO-friendly content strategies and offer their clients advice on how they can improve their search engine rankings.

6. Know how to negotiate fair rates and payment terms.

Start by researching industry standards for the type of work you're providing - this will give you an idea of a reasonable rate. Before negotiating, consider any unique project elements impacting your final rate, such as research time or specialized knowledge others may not possess.

When it comes time to discuss payment terms, be sure to thoroughly explain the scope of the project and any timelines that need to be met. Ensure both parties have agreed on these terms before beginning work so there are no misunderstandings once the project is completed. Also, consider whether you would prefer a one-time fee or milestone payments. Fee structures can depend on the type of project and your experience level.

For one-time fee structures, freelancers usually charge a flat rate for the entire project. This type of payment is most common for smaller tasks that don't require ongoing revisions or updates, such as logo design or web page building. It's also beneficial if you have limited time to complete the project and need to provide the client with a definite quote upfront. On the other hand, milestone payments are more suited to larger projects that require regular progress updates. This could include website development projects, copywriting assignments, or video production jobs that are broken down into stages. With this structure, freelancers receive part of their fees when certain tasks are completed and can revise their estimates as needed depending on how long it takes for each stage.

Knowing best practices when it comes to freelancing also helps during negotiations. Be aware that some clients may not hire based solely on cost. They may value quality and experience just as much as your writing fee. So, demonstrating your talent through previous projects and reviews is just as important as having a competitive rate. Having these conversations early in the process can help create clarity for both parties involved, making sure everyone knows their expectations for each other.

7. Prioritize cultivating personal branding.

Cultivating personal branding is an essential part of succeeding as a freelance writer. To stand out from the competition, it's important to take some time to reflect on your skills, passions and experiences and develop a unique narrative that sets you apart.

Creating a portfolio of your work is one way to show off your skills and demonstrate why people should hire you. Consider adding visuals and graphics in addition to text-based content, so potential clients can quickly get an overview of your capabilities. Additionally, being active on relevant social media channels can help establish yourself as an authority in the field and highlight recent projects or successes.

Networking with other freelancers, editors, publishers and industry professionals can also help create valuable connections that will be beneficial in the long run. Finally, take advantage of any speaking or mentoring opportunities that come your way - these are great ways to showcase your expertise while expanding your network at the same time. A well-rounded personal brand is key for positioning yourself as an expert in freelance writing.

8. Know when to turn down projects.

As a freelance writer, it's important to know when to turn down projects that don't align with your skill set, goals or values. It can be tempting to say yes to every project, especially when starting out, but staying true to yourself and your long-term career goals is important.

Saying 'Yes' to every project may seem like an easy way to make money in the short-term, but it can be detrimental in the long run. By sticking to projects that are relevant to your expertise and interests, you can ensure consistent quality output and build a good reputation for yourself. Additionally, turning down the occasional project will free up more time for you to take on other more lucrative opportunities that can help advance your career even further.

To learn when to say 'No,' start by ensuring you clearly understand what topics you are passionate about and which are off-limits. This will make it easier for you to recognize potential problems before they come up. You must also be mindful of any ethical considerations that may impact your decision. For example, working on projects related to controversial topics like politics or religion might make you uncomfortable if those views don't align with yours.

When deciding whether to take on a particular project, consider how much time and energy is involved compared to the level of financial and non-financial reward that it offers. Factor in benefits such as exposure or portfolio additions. If you find yourself second-guessing the project after considering these factors, it might be best to pass on the opportunity and focus your attention on projects that better align with your passions and values instead.

9. Set clearly defined and achievable goals.

Having clearly defined goals is essential for successfully managing your freelance writing career. A clear goal can act as a guide and help you stay focused on what's important, such as developing a strong portfolio, identifying target markets, and consistently producing high-quality content. Setting specific milestones can also serve as motivation and will help you stay motivated to keep pushing forward towards success. Additionally, having clearly defined goals can help you to stay organized and prioritize the tasks that are most important for achieving them.

Consider breaking your goals down into smaller, achievable steps that you can work on day by day. This will help keep you motivated and focused on progress, even when progress seems slow. Also, track your progress regularly - this will help you receive feedback and adjust as needed. Keeping track of the projects you are working on, the number of words written, and any other metrics relevant to your job can help you receive honest feedback and adjust your strategy accordingly. This can also help with focusing on the small details that will ultimately make a big difference in terms of quality and success. Additionally, regular progress checks can provide valuable insight into which new opportunities might be worth pursuing further.

It's also important to make sure that you have the financial and mental resources available to reach your goals. If monetary investments are necessary, research different funding options that could help cover costs associated with taking classes or buying equipment. When managing stress, be sure to create a healthy balance between work and personal life, so you don't become overwhelmed or burn out.

10. They don't let self-doubt hold them back.

Self-doubt can be one of the biggest roadblocks for freelancers to reach their full potential. It's only natural to have moments of insecurity about your abilities or feel like you're not good enough, but it's important to know that these doubts don't need to hold you back from achieving your goals.

Start by learning to identify these thoughts and then challenge them with positive affirmations. Remind yourself of all your successes and skills, and find ways to continue learning and growing to push yourself further. Speak with others who have faced similar feelings, or look for an inspiring mentor who can help guide you through moments of self-doubt.

An example of an individual overcoming self-doubt to become a success is Stephen King, the iconic horror author of novels like The Shining and IT. After being rejected by dozens of publishers and enduring years of struggle, King was finally able to break through with his 1974 novel Carrie and has since become one of the most successful authors in history. His story serves as a testament to the power of perseverance and highlights that even the most difficult odds can be overcome.

It's also important to believe in yourself - remember that success takes time and patience, so don't be too hard on yourself if progress isn't happening as fast as you'd like. If you ever feel overwhelmed, take a step back and give yourself some breathing room. Everything will come together in time if you continue taking the right steps toward your long-term objectives. With the right attitude, there is no limit to what you can achieve when self-doubt is not an issue holding you back.

Chapter 3 Choosing Your Perfect Writing Niche

Choosing a niche is important for freelance writers because it helps them focus their skills and knowledge on a specific area of expertise. By specializing in one particular industry or subject matter, you can more easily become an authority and build up your reputation as an expert. Furthermore, when potential clients are looking for someone to work with, having a clear understanding of your niche makes it easier for them to assess whether you are the right person to hire.

After years in business and the real estate industry, I fell into writing about this field. Combining my practical experience with my knack for the written word was a perfect combination, and I ended up finding a lucrative niche in commercial and investment real estate writing. It turns out that when you combine your practical expertise with your passion for writing, you can find a perfectly tailored niche for yourself that provides a great income year after year. Doing the research to find your particular market niche is key - when you manage to make those two elements fit together like pieces of a puzzle, you'll have found success.

The same experience can hold true for any consumer-related industry. It requires research and some hard work, but when you find a niche that combines your practical knowledge with your writing style and interests, it can pay off handsomely. Not only will this combination make it easier to write about topics related to that industry, but it can also help you stand out from the competition as an expert in a certain field.

The first step when picking a writing niche is to know yourself. Think about what motivates you most, as well as any unique skills or knowledge you bring to the table. This will help narrow down the field and make your search more efficient. Then, research potential niches by looking at current trends and what topics are in demand with possible audiences and paying clients.

Once you've found something that interests you, take time to study its ins and outs so that you understand both the challenge and potential of it being a successful niche for you. Finally, trust your instincts when making a decision. If something feels wrong or fear of failure sets in, take a step back and consider other options.

8 Ways To Choose Your Perfect Writing Niche

If you're a freelance writer looking for ways to differentiate yourself from the competition and establish a successful writing career, then one of the most important steps you should take is choosing your perfect writing niche.

Choosing your perfect writing niche can be a game-changer for freelance writers because by taking the time to research and identify a niche, they can gain an edge over their competitors. It demonstrates that you are an expert in a particular area who understands the industry's current trends and how to target certain markets effectively. Having this unique perspective allows you to create content that stands out from the rest and maximizes your chances of success as a online writer.

You can easily identify a specialty that reflects your skillset and interests with the right knowledge and approach. Here are eight tips to help you narrow your search and find the perfect writing niche.

1. Identify Your Skills

Take time to consider your skills and talents carefully. Ask yourself: What am I good at? What do I enjoy writing about? What types of projects have been successful for me in the past? Also, consider what topics you might be interested in exploring during your freelance career. It's important to choose a niche you are passionate about and can easily write compelling content for. Once you know what skills, interests, and experiences make up your ideal niche, you'll be prepared to become a successful writer.

In addition to honing in on the type of clients or projects that would work best for you, setting yourself apart from other writers is also key. Think about ways you can showcase your unique skills to potential clients. Do you have a specialty in SEO writing or marketing? What other qualities do you bring to the table that make you stand out in the freelance copywriting world? Take stock of your skills and experiences and use them to your advantage when building a successful freelance career.

2. Do Your Research

Doing your research is essential if you want to find the perfect writing niche. Start by perusing the web and noting what topics are currently being discussed – you can use this as a starting point for identifying trends and potential audiences. Additionally, look out for job postings from possible paying clients - this will give you an idea of which topics are highly demanded in the current market.

Once you've narrowed down your choices, read up on potential niches and gain a better understanding of their ins and outs, their challenges and the potential they have to be successful. Pay attention to information such as the goal of each project or article, any special requirements that must be met, who the intended audience is and how much competition there may be in that area.

In addition to online resources, consider reaching out to other writers who focus on similar topics for further insight - working with them also serves as an excellent opportunity for networking. Finally, when researching potential niches, remember to keep track of all your findings so that they're easily accessible when it comes time to make a decision – after all, knowledge is power.

3. Consider What Motivates You

When considering which niche to focus on, remember to consider what motivates you the most. Ask yourself questions like, 'Why am I drawn to this particular topic?' or 'What aspects of this work excite me?'.

Your interests and motivations should go beyond simply wanting to make money. While financial incentives are beneficial, they shouldn't be the sole reason for your choice. Instead, select something that truly sparks your passion because that is more likely to keep you inspired even after long work hours.

In addition, look for challenges that come with each project. If something feels too easy, it won't allow you to grow as a writer. Also, consider how much freedom you have when expressing your ideas and opinions. Your ability to express yourself freely is critical in any writing-based job. Lastly, consider which type of audience your work will be catered to and how comfortable you feel engaging with them. The best writers understand their reader's needs and desires, so this information is essential when researching prospective niches.

4. Take Note of Current Trends

It's important to stay up-to-date with the current trends when picking a niche for your writing career. Paying attention to the topics being discussed online and in traditional media can help you identify potential projects and provide useful insight into relevant communities or audiences.

In recent years, topics such as sustainability, artificial intelligence and cryptocurrency have become increasingly popular. These areas often present intriguing opportunities for freelance writers to create content around the concept of taking advantage of a new technology or movement in order to tell stories that can engage and inspire readers. Additionally, many people are now turning towards e-learning platforms such as Udemy to gain a more comprehensive understanding of certain subjects and industries. Exploring these contemporary trends can help any writer identify their perfect writing niche.

Furthermore, watching for new developments or changes within your chosen field will help ensure your content is always fresh and interesting. Not only will this help draw in readers, but it will also allow you to stay ahead of other writers in terms of knowledge and expertise. Similarly, familiarizing yourself with emerging trends can offer you valuable growth opportunities. You can push your skillset and expand into new areas by taking on challenging projects related to these topics.

5. Earnings Potential

When researching potential niches, it's important to consider the potential earning potential of each option. Knowing how much money you can potentially make from a particular sub-niche or topic will help you determine whether it is viable for your career in the long run.

A sub-niche is a narrower subject within a larger niche. For example, if the general niche is "Business Writing," then some sub-niches could be "Copywriting for Startups" or "B2B Email Copywriting." Other examples of sub-niches could be "Sports Journalism" or "Healthy Lifestyle Blogging" under the broader niche of "Writing." Sub-niches allow you to focus your attention on specific topics and gain an even better understanding of their potential.

It's also worth considering whether there is any barrier to entry. If you're dealing with topics requiring specialized knowledge or skills, this might result in higher earnings but could leave you at a competitive disadvantage. Similarly, understanding the competition in your chosen niche can help you decide whether it's worth pursuing or whether it might be better to focus on an alternative topic. Additionally, identifying key players within the industry can give you useful insight into what strategies have been successful for them and which monetization methods are likely to yield the best results for you.

Lastly, don't forget about factors like scalability. Scalability is important when selecting a niche or sub-niche for freelance writing. It refers to the ability to expand and grow your income potential within that particular field as you become more experienced and knowledgeable. When picking a niche, it's important to think about how much potential there is for you to explore different topics and develop new ideas in the future.

For example, if you're interested in content marketing, you could focus on a sub-niche like "SEO copywriting" or "Social Media Copywriting." These topics allow you to explore different types of platforms and target audiences, which can expand your income potential over time. Additionally, understanding how SEO works and keeping up with algorithm changes can help you stay ahead of the competition.

Similarly, learning about social media trends and analytics will allow you to create more effective campaigns that reach wider audiences. These strategies are essential for maximizing scalability within the content marketing niche. On the other hand, if the earning potential of your chosen niche is limited, you may need to look for additional sources of income to sustain your writing career.

6. Connect With Other Writers

When reaching out to writers in similar niches, ask open-ended questions such as what strategies they use when tackling new projects or how they manage their time when handling multiple tasks. An open-ended question cannot be answered with a simple yes or no, encouraging the respondent to give a longer, more detailed answer.

This allows you to get to know them personally and gives you a chance to gain valuable insight into their unique approach. Additionally, don't forget to inquire about their own experience within the industry. By listening carefully to their stories and perspectives, you'll gain invaluable advice and knowledge from those who have been there before.

By building relationships with other writers and tapping into their expertise and experience, everybody stands to benefit. It will allow them to hone their craft, collaborate with like-minded individuals, and give you a chance to learn from those who have come before you.

7. Test Out Potential Niches

Trying out different niches is a great way to gain experience and insights into various writing styles without committing long-term. For many new writers, this experimentation allows them to see what type of content resonates with their readers or which sub-niches they might be particularly interested in.

When testing out potential niches, it's important to remember that it's not all about the money. Although financial considerations are certainly important, don't forget to also consider other aspects, such as whether you're enjoying the writing process itself and if your passion lies within the particular field. Additionally, don't be afraid to take some risks. Even if a topic or genre doesn't seem worth exploring at first glance, you may be surprised by what hidden gems lie beneath the surface if you give it a chance.

Finally, always remember that success in any field requires hard work and dedication. No matter how promising your chosen niche seems, don't expect miracles from day one. Be sure to put in the required effort and set realistic goals that can be achieved gradually over time. With these factors in mind, there's no reason why experimentation shouldn't help new writers gain an invaluable understanding of different writing styles and pave the path to future success.

8. Trust Yourself & Follow Your Gut Instincts

Following your intuition is essential when deciding on a writing niche. Although researching related topics and gaining advice from professionals can be extremely beneficial, it's up to you to decide which works best for you. Putting trust in yourself and taking risks are both important factors that must be considered, since often the most rewarding results come from those who dare to be bold.

When making decisions regarding your writing niche, don't be afraid to explore new terrain and push yourself outside your comfort zone. Taking risks can open up a world of profitable possibilities. By venturing into unfamiliar territory and trying out different styles or topics, you may discover hidden talents that were previously unknown. Additionally, listening closely to your gut instincts despite external pressures or expectations can also help lead you toward success. If something seems like a good fit for you, go ahead and give it a try.

How To Choose a Recession-Resistant Niche To Write About

A recession-proof or recession-resistant business is resilient and can weather an economic downturn. These businesses are essential, provide necessary services, or have a product that people cannot do without.

Choosing a recession-resistant niche to write about can seem like a formidable task, especially in the ever-changing climate of our current world economy. However, with research and focus, it is possible to identify which topics and niches can survive through all economic cycles.

The first step in finding a recession-proof niche is to analyze current trends. What topics are most often discussed, and what remains relevant even during economic troubles? This can be done through online tools such as keyword trackers and market research reports. Additionally, reading recent news articles and industry publications can help you understand the current business climate.

Once you have identified general trends within your chosen niche, you can dive deeper into the individual subject matter and consider those that have the potential for long-term success despite the ebbs and flows of the economy. Popular topics include health & wellness, green initiatives, technology advancements, finances, education opportunities, entertainment & lifestyle changes. These topics tend to remain relevant no matter what stage the economy is in, as they address issues important to all people regardless of their financial situation.

Finally, as you narrow down your list of potential writing niches, ensure each topic interests you personally. Doing so will help keep your enthusiasm intact even when times feel tough, or sales start dropping off due to economic uncertainty. With the right combination of knowledge and passion for your writing subject matter, you'll be able to find success during even the roughest times.

To help with your search, here's a list of 99 businesses and services that at in demand and perform fairly well no matter how good or bad the economy is, listed in alphabetical order:

1. Accounting firms
2. Airport shuttle
3. Alternative energy sources
4. Animal control officers
5. Animal rescues
6. Appliance repair shops
7. Armored car personnel
8. Auction houses
9. Auto mechanics/repair shops
10. Banking
11. Bed & breakfast hosts
12. Book stores
13. Bouncy castle hire companies
14. Car rental companies
15. Car sales
16. Casino workers
17. Caterers
18. Cell phone providers
19. Certified Public Accountants
20. Cleaning services
21. Clothes dry cleaning businesses
22. Computer technology specialists
23. Construction materials and equipment suppliers
24. Copywriters & technical writers
25. Courier services
26. Data entry specialists

27. Daycare centers and kindergartens
28. Delivery services
29. Department stores
30. Disc jockeys
31. Donut or coffee shop owners
32. Drone pilots
33. E-commerce
34. Educational institutions
35. Elderly care and home health aides
36. Event planners
37. Fast food restaurants
38. Financial planning
39. Florists
40. Freelance web developers
41. Funeral homes
42. Gardeners
43. Gas stations
44. Government offices
45. Graphic designers
46. Groceries and food stores
47. Hairdressers
48. Handymen
49. Hardware stores
50. Healthcare and medical services
51. Home entertainment installers
52. Home improvement stores
53. Home repair contractors
54. Home security systems
55. Homesteading
56. House sitting
57. Insurance companies
58. Landscaping businesses

59. Law firms
60. Libraries
61. Locksmiths
62. Maintenance services
63. Manufacturing
64. Moving companies
65. Music stores
66. Musical instrument instructors
67. News journalists & editors
68. Notary Publics
69. Online retailers
70. Online tutoring
71. Permaculture
72. Personal trainers
73. Pest control companies
74. Pet care services
75. Pharmaceuticals
76. Pharmacies
77. Plumbers/electricians/HVAC technicians
78. Postal services
79. Printing companies
80. Private detectives
81. Professional organizers
82. Professional photographers
83. Property management
84. Real estate agents/brokers
85. Security guards
86. Solar energy
87. Solar panel installation
88. Sporting goods stores
89. Sports writers & bloggers
90. Tattoo artists

91. Tax consultants
92. Telecommunications providers
93. Tour guides
94. Translators
95. Travel agents
96. Turf maintenance
97. Utilities (water, gas, electricity)
98. Veterinarian assistants
99. Veterinarians

There you have it! Nearly one hundred businesses and services that are recession-proof. These businesses do relatively well regardless of the economy being good or bad. So, consider one of these niche options to start your freelance writing career or expand your practice. With the right amount of skill and a little bit of luck, they should provide you with a steady stream of income and clients year after year.

What Is a Sub-Niche and Why Do They Matter?

As a freelance writer, it is important to understand the difference between a niche and a sub-niche to maximize your income and attract high-paying clients. A niche is a large category or topic in which an individual specializes, such as "web design" or "fashion marketing." On the other hand, a sub-niche is an even more specific field within the larger niche, such as "e-commerce web design" or "luxury fashion marketing."

By specializing in a sub-niche rather than just the general niche topic, it can be easier for freelance writers to gain valuable clients by showcasing their expertise in that particular area of specialization. Specializing also helps freelance writers maximize their income potential by providing more specialized services that clients may be unable to find among generalists.

Sub-niches are also advantageous because they allow freelance writers to hone their skills within a narrower area. This makes them more desirable to existing customers who may require deeper knowledge on the subject than what would be offered by someone with only basic familiarity. With this comes higher pay for those who have mastered their chosen sub-niche: clients know that well-informed professionals bring added value to their projects and are willing to pay accordingly.

For example, let's say you specialize in content creation for health & wellness websites. Within this niche you could further specialize into sub-niches like vegan nutrition, sports medicine, or medical aesthetics. Each of these sub-specialties requires its own unique set of skills and knowledge. For example, vegan nutrition requires up-to-date knowledge of plant-based diets, while medical aesthetics requires familiarity with different treatments and procedures. So, taking on projects within these areas can help you develop your proficiency faster and generate greater earnings from highly specialized services that few others can provide.

You can even drive-down into a sub-niche by creating additional sub-niches. Using vegan nutrition as an example, we can come up with plant-based meal ideas, nutritional supplementation advice, vegan beauty and lifestyle tips, vegan fitness advice, vegan food alternatives, and vegan travel guides.

Additionally, when developing content for a particular sub-niche market, it can be beneficial to become active online in communities dedicated to that specific topic. Doing so will help you stay current on industry news & trends and make valuable connections with potential customers looking for experienced professionals with firsthand knowledge of the subject matter.

Freelancers may succeed more when they choose a specialized sub-niche instead of offering generic services across all topics related to their main niches. There is a better potential for higher pay, and one's credentials will stand out more among other professionals due to specialized experience and insight into the chosen study area.

Now let's conduct an experiment. Take the recession-resilient niches previously discussed and try to come up with 5 different sub-niches for each niche. Here are a few to get you started, along with some that weren't previously listed:

Accounting firms

- Business accounting

- Personal accounting

Airport shuttle

- Airport pickup and drop off services

- Intercity transfers between airports

Alternative energy sources

- Solar energy

- Wind power

Animal control officers

- Wildlife rescues & relocation services

- Exotic animal capture & containment services

Animal rescues

- Dog rescue and rehabilitation centers

- Cat rescue and adoption centers

Appliance repair shops

- Refrigerator repair businesses

- Washer/Dryer repair businesses

Armored car personnel

- Cash delivery services

- Money transport services

Auction houses

- Online auction companies

- Onsite auction companies

Auto mechanics/repair shops

- Automobile engine maintenance and repairs

- Car body repair & painting services

Banking

- Local bank branches

- International banking institutions

Bed & breakfast hosts

- Urban B&B's with modern amenities

- Rural B&B's with natural views and attractions

Book stores

- Independent bookstores

- Chain bookstores

Bouncy castle hire companies

- Outdoor inflatable party rentals

- Indoor inflatable party rentals

Car rental companies

- Airport car hire services

- Local city car sharing services

Car sales

- Used cars dealerships

- New cars dealerships

Casino workers

- Poker dealer staff

- Slot machine attendants

Caterers

- Large scale corporate event catering services

- Private party catering services

Cell phone providers

- Prepaid and postpaid plans from international carriers

- Carrier deals for unlocked phones & tablets

Certified Public Accountants (CPAs)

- Tax preparation & filing services

- Financial consulting & planning services

Cleaning services

- Commercial office cleaning businesses

- Residential home cleaning businesses

Community centers

- Day care facilities & programs

- living assistance& support services

Courier services

- Same day delivery services

- Overnight package delivery services

Dairy farmers

- Milk production & distribution companies

- Cheese production & distribution companies

Delivery drivers

- Food delivery services

- Grocery delivery services

Dentists

- General dentistry offices

- Pediatric dental offices

Department stores

- High end boutiques and specialty stores

- Chain department stores

Electricians

- Residential electrical wiring & repairs

- Commercial electrical installations & maintenance services

Financial advisors

- Retirement planning and investment services

- Debt consolidation and credit repair services

Florists

- Flower delivery services

- Bouquet arrangement services

Gardeners/landscapers

- Lawn mowing & yard care businesses

- Tree trimming & shrub pruning businesses

Grocery stores

- Small family owned grocery stores

- Large chain supermarkets

Home health aides

- Non-medical in home assistance

- Nursing care & medical assistance services

Hotels/motels

- Boutique hotels & resorts

- Budget friendly motels

Insurance agents

- Auto insurance policies and coverage plans

- Health insurance policies and coverage plans

Janitors/building cleaners

- Industrial & commercial cleaning businesses

- Post construction cleanup services

Jewelers

- Premium jewelry retailers

- Discount jewelry stores

Landlords/property owners

- Residential property management services

- Commercial property leasing & management services

Lawyers

- Family law attorneys

- Criminal defense lawyers

Librarians

- Public library services

- School library aides

Marketers/advertisers

- Content marketing agencies

- Paid media contract positions

Mechanics/technicians

- Heavy equipment repair businesses

- Computer and electronics repair services

Moving companies

- Long distance moving services

- Local moving & packing services

Office managers/administrators

- Corporate office administrators

- Small business office managers

Personal trainers

- Group fitness instructors

- One-on-one personal training sessions

Pet groomers/sitters

- Dog grooming services

- Pet sitting & walking services

Pharmacists

- Independent pharmacy owners

- Chain pharmacy employees

Real estate agents/brokers

- Commercial real estate brokers

- Residential real estate agents

Retail salespeople

- Luxury retail boutiques

- Discount department stores

Security guards/systems

- High security corporate facility guards

- Home security systems installation services

Teachers/tutors

- K-12 teachers

- University and college professors

Tour guides/travel agents

- Cultural attraction tour guides

- International travel agents

Veterinarians

- Animal hospital doctors

- Pet emergency clinics

Web designers/developers

- Freelance website design & development services

- Ecommerce web platform development companies

Coming up with sub-niches for a particular topic is limited only by one's imagination. Once you have developed an understanding of the broader area you are writing about, it is just a matter of exploring the possibilities and narrowing down which topics best suit your strengths and interests. There is no limit to the number of sub-niches that can be created or explored. Everything from health and nutrition to art and travel could be discussed in relation to your chosen niche. For any writer, the sky is truly the limit when it comes to selecting topics to write about!

Chapter 4 Why Work for Cheap? How To Find Clients Who Are Willing To Pay What You're Worth

Working for cheap can be a tempting proposition, especially in the beginning stages of a freelancing career. After all, extra money – no matter how little – is often better than no money at all.

To be fair, there may be some short-term benefits of working for cheap in the beginning stages of a freelancing career, such as gaining experience, building a portfolio and starting to build relationships within an industry. It's important to remember, however, that this path is not always sustainable or beneficial in the long run. Working for cheap devalues your skills and services and can prevent you from earning money commensurate with the quality of your work. Not only will you have less time and energy to devote to higher-paying assignments, but your reputation as an experienced freelancer may precede you and scare away potential customers willing to pay more for your services. This can lead to burnout and dissatisfaction over time, which is why it's essential to find a balance between offering competitive rates and providing the best service possible.

So, the six-figure question becomes, "How can you avoid working for cheap?" The answer lies in finding clients interested in investing their resources into your expertise. To do this, you must market yourself correctly using platforms like Upwork, LinkedIn, or specialized job boards. Put together a portfolio of past work from well-known clients and showcase the value you offer by highlighting awards, certifications, or any other relevant achievements that make you stand out from the rest of the crowd.

Another way to boost your appeal to potential clients is by offering discounts for repeat business or payment plans for larger projects, such as book writing. Doing so shows that you understand their commitments when hiring someone, and you are willing to provide them with more flexibility throughout the process. As a freelance professional, establishing trust with clients is key. If they know they can trust you with their reputation and finances, they will be more likely to invest those resources into projects involving you.

Finally, networking should never be underestimated. Utilizing contacts in the industry can go a long way – whether through word-of-mouth references or even just striking up casual conversations with interesting people at events or conferences related to your field of expertise. These connections often lead to business opportunities and advice from industry experts, which can prove invaluable if used properly.

12 Tips for Finding Awesome Clients

While it can be tricky to find clients who are willing to pay you what you're worth as a writer, it's definitely not impossible. Here are some tips for finding those dream clients:

1. Don't be afraid to work with difficult clients - sometimes they just need some guidance and patience to understand the value of your work.

Working with difficult clients can be a challenging and sometimes discouraging experience, but it doesn't have to be. With the right approach and attitude, difficult clients can become long-term customers who are more than willing to pay for quality work.

One reason why a client may be difficult to work with is if they are trying to multi-task. For example, a content manager at a large company or agency often has many responsibilities and relies on freelance writers to produce content quickly and efficiently. In these cases, the client may forget that the freelancer is just one person and expect more than what is realistically possible in terms of turnaround time. Additionally, the client may not provide detailed instructions or be open to feedback about their requests, resulting in frustration and confusion for both parties.

Patience and understanding are key to building a successful relationship with difficult clients. It's important to listen carefully to their needs and address any issues they may have without becoming frustrated or impatient. Taking the time to explain your process in detail is also helpful. This gives the client a better understanding of what type of work you do and how their investment will yield a result that meets their expectations.

Another way to build trust between yourself and difficult clients is by keeping them updated throughout the project. Providing regular updates on progress helps keep those "difficult" moments at bay by assuring the client that you are working diligently towards meeting their goals. Additionally, documentation outlining each step of your process will help clear any misunderstandings that may arise during your collaboration.

Finally, don't be afraid to acknowledge when something isn't going as planned or if revisions need to be made. Transparency is essential in establishing a trusting relationship between yourself and any client, regardless of how easy or difficult they may be. Also, remember that not all difficult clients are created equal. Some may just need more guidance or help in understanding the value of your services, while others may simply be trying to get as much out of you for as little as possible.

2. Consider working with agencies instead of individual clients - they often have higher budgets and may be more

willing to pay for quality writing.

Working with agencies can be a great way for freelance writers to get their foot in the door and expand their client base. Agencies often have larger budgets and more resources available than individual clients, which means there is a greater potential for higher pay. In addition, agencies tend to be more organized and have clear expectations regarding how work should be completed. This professional approach makes it easier for freelance writers to produce quality content within an established timeline.

Agency-based projects can also allow freelancers to gain exposure and build connections within their field of expertise. Working with different companies on one campaign or project allows freelancers to explore new strategies while learning from experienced professionals and gaining valuable industry insights they may not have had access to through individual clients. Additionally, agencies often work with multiple clients simultaneously, meaning there is a greater potential for additional projects if your work meets the required standards.

Finally, working with agencies can open doors to other opportunities, such as writing contract positions or in-house roles, typically with more stable income and longer contracts. This allows freelance writers to advance their careers by transitioning from project-by-project assignments into more permanent positions with higher earning potentials.

3. Don't discount smaller clients - even if their budget is limited, they may have a lot of potential for long-term projects and referrals.

Although it may be tempting to focus on larger clients with more generous budgets, freelance writers should not discount the value of working with smaller clients. Even if a client's budget is limited, they can still provide plenty of potential for long-term projects and referrals.

First, working with small businesses can be an excellent opportunity to build experience. Smaller projects typically require less time and effort, allowing freelancers to work quickly and refine their skills in different areas. Additionally, making connections with these smaller clients can lead to bigger opportunities down the line. Many larger companies are willing to trust smaller businesses' recommendations as they share similar values and goals.

Another benefit of working with small businesses is that there may be room for flexibility regarding pricing and deadlines. Often, these organizations may need help finishing a project but do not have the funds to pay a full rate upfront or meet tight timelines. As such, offering an hourly rate or providing payment plans could be ways in which freelancers make the process more manageable for both parties involved. Not only does this result in satisfied customers but also possibly further collaboration on future projects.

Last but not least, small businesses often refer other companies looking for services similar to those you offer. This means you increase your chances of building new customer relationships by nurturing relationships with smaller clients. So don't overlook small businesses when searching for new opportunities. Even if their budget is limited, they may have great potential for long-term projects and referrals.

4. Always lead with your strengths and experience, and don't hesitate to negotiate for higher pay if the project warrants it.

When pitching yourself to potential employers, it is important to demonstrate how your skills and experience align with their project needs and explain why you are the right fit for the job. Be sure to showcase any relevant prior work and provide details about what sets you apart from other candidates. This is also an opportunity to negotiate for higher pay. If a client requires more sophisticated work beyond what was initially discussed, there's no harm in asking for additional compensation if the project warrants it.

One tactic I like to use is a phrase such as "The fee I currently receive from clients with projects such as yours is $X." This wording implies a couple of things. First, the prospective client is being told that others are willing to step up to the plate and pay my asking price. Second, the potential client is being told that they are in a competitive situation.

Leading with your strengths and negotiating for higher payment can also open up doors to long-term projects or even in-house positions down the road. Showcasing your capabilities through successful negotiations and delivering quality results sets you up for future collaborations with clients who appreciate and value your expertise and respect your negotiating skills. Not only does this increase your earning potential, but it also provides more stability while allowing freelancers to take their careers further.

5. Network within your industry and get recommendations from satisfied clients.

Networking is an essential part of a successful freelance writing career. Connecting with other professionals in your industry and keeping up with the latest trends can open up new opportunities and help you stay informed. Additionally, getting recommendations from satisfied clients can be an invaluable way to build credibility and recognition.

First, join writing groups on social media platforms and attend webinars or virtual conferences related to writing and publishing. These communities are great places to learn about new topics, get feedback on your work, and connect with people with similar interests.

Additionally, networking events such as writers' conferences are great places to meet other professionals in person. Having face-to-face conversations can create meaningful relationships that may lead to more projects.

Another way to network within the freelance writing industry is by attending seminars or workshops related to the niches you specialize in. This provides valuable insight into what editors are looking for and allows you to interact with potential employers interested in hiring freelancers for specific projects.

Finally, don't forget about the importance of word-of-mouth referrals. Word-of-mouth referrals are important because they provide a reliable way for freelancers to build their reputation and reach a larger audience. Word-of-mouth referrals are often more trusted than paid advertisements or other marketing efforts, as they come from people who have had firsthand experience working with a freelancer. Additionally, many clients prefer to work with freelancers who have been referred by someone they know and trust. Referrals also provide an opportunity for freelance writers to network and interact with new clients, as referrals often originate from colleagues or peers in the industry.

So, don't hesitate to ask your satisfied clients for recommendations after completing a successful project. Many happy customers will be willing to connect their contacts with skilled freelancers like yourself. Networking within your industry and getting recommendations from satisfied clients is key for any freelance writer looking to build their portfolio and expand their client base.

6. Keep an eye out for job postings that list a specific budget or rate.

Being able to identify comparable opportunities can be beneficial in helping you determine the scope of your project and make sure you are getting paid what you are worth. Knowing the budget before entering into negotiations can also help you figure out if you have the resources and skill set necessary to execute the job.

When looking for projects with a specific budget or rate, be sure to read through the details carefully. Many times, clients will list a range or average instead of giving an exact amount. This could mean they are willing to pay more than the listed rate, depending on your credentials and experience. Additionally, understanding client expectations is key when submitting your proposal. Ensure they understand how much work is involved upfront, so there are no surprises further down the line.

It's also important to factor in any additional costs associated with the project, such as research time, travel expenses, or other miscellaneous fees. This way, when it comes time to negotiate payment terms, both parties know exactly what services are being rendered and agree on an appropriate fee. With careful consideration and thoughtful negotiation skills, freelance writers can ensure they receive fair compensation for their work while providing clients with quality results.

7. Be open to trying new industries or niches where your skills may be in high demand.

It can be beneficial to keep an open mind and be willing to explore new industries or niches that may not have been on your radar. Identifying untapped opportunities can be a great way to expand your portfolio and find work in industries with high demand for talented writers.

There are many ways for freelancers to discover these new opportunities.

First, research and look into different industries you might want to work in. For example, if you specialize in copywriting, you could look into working in tech, finance, or healthcare – all of these fields typically require experienced writers with specialized knowledge. Additionally, follow industry experts on social media platforms like Twitter, LinkedIn, or Facebook – they often share leads and job postings relevant to their niche, which could lead to more project opportunities.

Second, attend networking events related to these industries to get acquainted with potential employers actively looking for skilled freelancers. Additionally, hosting your own meet-ups is a great way for other professionals within the same niche to connect. This will help grow your network and expose you to more projects that need doing.

Finally, don't underestimate the power of referrals. Ask clients from previous projects if they know someone who might need similar services. Word-of-mouth referrals are invaluable for finding quality work within various industries and niches.

8. Focus on building ongoing relationships with a few select clients rather than constantly searching for new ones.

As a freelance writer, establishing strong relationships with a few select clients can be advantageous in the long run. It allows you to hone your skills and create meaningful work and will also help ensure a steady income stream. When searching for new projects, try to find "ideal" clients who would benefit from your services and expertise. These people would use your services on an ongoing basis instead of those looking for one-off tasks.

Focus on delivering high-quality work for these ideal clients and make sure you communicate regularly with them. For instance, you could send weekly updates about the project status, provide feedback on their expectations, or simply check in and find out how things are going – this helps strengthen and maintain the relationship over time. Additionally, providing added value, such as extra advice or support, can set you apart from other freelancers in their eyes.

One great way to ensure successful client relationships is by creating long-term contracts which lay out the scope of work and payment terms upfront. This ensures everyone knows exactly what is expected of them, which can prevent any disputes or misunderstandings further down the line. Finally, taking innovative approaches to problem-solving can go a long way towards winning loyal customers who will come back time again when they need assistance with writing projects.

However, as important as it is to focus on building relationships with select clients, it's also important for freelance writers to diversify their income streams. Having multiple sources of revenue helps ensure that your livelihood as a freelancer isn't dependent on just one or two clients. Sure, it takes more time and effort upfront to find new projects, but this approach can help provide financial stability and freedom in the long run.

Make sure to explore different platforms or networks where you can actively search for job opportunities. Doing so will allow you to expand your portfolio and capitalize on untapped markets which may be looking for talented writers. Additionally, having a great online presence, such as a website with regular blog posts, makes it easier for people to reach out and inquire about your services. Establishing yourself as an authority in the field can help attract more business prospects that could turn into ideal clients and repeat business.

9. Explore freelance marketplaces or bidding sites, but beware of undervaluing yourself in the scramble for jobs.

These sites can often attract individuals looking to get writing services at a discounted rate. As a result, you should always make sure to have an understanding of the going rates in your field before submitting a bid on any project. Making sure that you're not working for too little is essential if you want to ensure that you can remain profitable in freelancing.

One of the key strategies to ensure profitability in freelancing is to set realistic and competitive fees. If you quote too low, it could affect your ability to pay bills and impact any future prospects if you develop a reputation as an "affordable" (i.e., cheap) freelancer. Considering all factors when determining rates, such as experience level, project size, and timeline, is important.

Calculate your estimated hours for a given task and factor in overhead costs or additional expenses for necessary resources, then determine your mark-up. This can help you develop a rate that allows you to remain profitable while also understanding the value of your work. Always be transparent with your clients about payment terms and timeframes. Having a clear agreement from the start will ensure expectations are met on both sides.

Additionally, take the time to research different types of project contracts or engagements before accepting anything on these marketplaces. There could be hidden costs or surprises you weren't expecting, such as platform transaction fees, so it's always best to be prepared. On top of that, these sites often contain multiple writers who are competing against each other for the same job. Having the edge over the competition, such as offering additional services or having a strong portfolio, can help increase your chances of landing the project.

Finally, while many freelance marketplaces offer reliable opportunities and good pay rates, beware of taking jobs with clients you do not trust or have a bad reputation from other freelancers. This could hurt your career in the long run due to potential missed deadlines, unsatisfactory results, or bad reviews. Weighing both sides is necessary when deciding whether or not this route is right for you - explore freelance marketplaces but don't compromise by undervaluing yourself.

10. Offer package deals or bundled services to make your rates more appealing.

Packages help with convenience, as they often solve a single problem for one fee without the client worrying about individual costs. By bundling your services together, you can reduce your overall cost while maintaining an appropriate rate attractive to potential clients. Packaging is also beneficial in terms of pricing structure. Instead of asking the client to pay multiple fees, offer a single flat rate to meet their needs. This approach can help avoid the client feel they are being "nickel and dimed."

Package deals can also be customized based on client preferences and needs. You could offer different packages at different costs catering to any budget range. For example, some clients may want a basic package with just the essential services, whereas others may opt for a more comprehensive bundle with additional features or extras that meet specific project requirements, such as keyword analysis or formatting for WordPress.

Furthermore, offering packages or bundled services is also beneficial from a marketing perspective. It helps establish your brand as an expert in the field and demonstrates your commitment to providing high-quality products and results. That being said, try not to overcrowd your offerings. Prospective clients should have two or three choices available so they don't feel overwhelmed when deciding. Overall, creating packages or bundles is a great way to make your rates more appealing while still providing value in your work.

11. Don't give in to desperation - it's better to wait for the right opportunity than settle for less than you deserve.

It can be tempting to accept any job offer that comes your way, especially in a difficult financial situation. However, it's important to remember that desperation often leads to settling for less than you deserve, which can have far-reaching implications, such as developing a reputation as a cheap content creator. Remember, sometimes waiting for the right opportunity is better than jumping at the first one – the outcome could be much more profitable and beneficial in the long run.

Taking time to evaluate a potential job or project can help you ensure you're getting compensated fairly and not selling yourself short. Researching what's available in the market can give you an idea of where your skills and experience fit in when it comes to pricing rates. Additionally, analyzing other projects and services offered by freelancers or agencies similar to yours will allow you to understand better how much your work is worth in the eyes of the client. As a result, you'll be in a stronger position to confidently negotiate contracts commensurate with your experience level.

Don't forget, there is always another opportunity just around the corner – so don't feel pressured into taking a job offered at lower pay or with unfavorable terms. If you're patient and willing to invest some effort into finding the right job that pays well for what you do, it will be worth it in the end.

12. Stay confident in your abilities and don't give up - the right client will come along eventually!

It can be disheartening not to see immediate results for the hard work that you put into building a business or freelance career, especially when it comes to finding the right clients. It's important to remember, however, that staying confident in your abilities and not giving up is key.

Focusing on honing your craft and continually developing your skills is essential. This practice will ensure you're ready when that ideal client opportunity arises. Put yourself out there: attend industry events and conferences, sign up for online marketplaces, and create engaging content on social media. All of these can help you make vital connections with people who may eventually become clients.

Above all, always believe in yourself and trust your abilities. Don't be discouraged if things don't happen as quickly as you would like because every successful journey takes time. It may take longer than expected to find a project or get hired by a company, but it's important to remain resilient and continue pushing forward until you do.

Chapter 5 Landing Your First Writing Gig: 10 Steps for Beginners

As a freelance writer, I remember the nervous excitement of landing my very first gig. I was eager to use my skills and prove myself as a valuable asset to a client. Unfortunately, that first project didn't go as smoothly as planned. The agency I worked with failed to disclose they were running the show, and as a result, my contact wasn't entirely sure what the client wanted. Needless to say, there were a few bumps in the road before we figured it all out.

But, as they say, every cloud has a silver lining. This experience made me realize just how in-demand my particular skill set was. It was a valuable lesson that helped me recognize the importance of doing my own due diligence before taking on a project. I learned to ask more questions upfront and to ensure that I had a solid understanding of the client's needs before beginning any work.

Now, as a seasoned freelancer with years of experience, I'm excited to share my hard-won knowledge with other aspiring writers. In this chapter, I'll share my top 10 tips for landing that all-important first writing gig, helping you navigate the process with confidence and ease. Whether you're new to the game or a seasoned pro, these tips are sure to help you elevate your freelance writing career to the next level.

1. Build a strong portfolio by writing sample pieces and creating a website to showcase your work.

Building a strong portfolio is essential to success in any writing or creative field. Writing sample pieces and creating a website are two of the most important steps freelancers should take when building their portfolio.

Writing sample pieces can allow potential clients to evaluate your writing style, tone, and ability. It also allows them to understand how you approach topics and what kind of work you can do for them. This self-promotion will often lead to more clients and opportunities for work. Having samples that showcase the range of your abilities will give those who may hire you an idea of how flexible you can be when it comes to working on various projects.

Creating a professional website is also key to building up a successful portfolio. Not only does this allow potential employers to get an immediate sense of who you are as a writer, but it also helps show off your best work and highlight any awards or accolades you may have received for past pieces. Your website should include sections devoted to showcasing your skills, listing previous projects, displaying any awards or certificates, and outlining your services. Additionally, you can feature media such as videos or audio clips that can help make potential employers even more interested in hiring you.

2. Network with fellow writers and professionals in the industry through online communities or local events.

Networking is essential if you want to make a name for yourself in any industry, and the writing field is no exception. Connecting with other writers and professionals in the industry can help you significantly when securing your first client.

Building relationships with people with more experience in this field will give you valuable insight into how to navigate the professional writing world. It also allows you to make connections that could potentially lead to job opportunities down the line. Furthermore, being part of a community of like-minded individuals who understand the ins and outs of writing can provide emotional support during what may be an intimidating process for newcomers to the craft.

In addition to gaining industry knowledge, networking helps writers build relationships with potential employers or peers that could open up new doors when looking for work. Being involved in these events might make it easier for employers to take notice of you, even before any work samples or pitches are sent their way. These connections may even help you land freelance projects without ever having to submit a work sample or pitch yourself directly.

3. Understand the different types of writing gigs available, from content creation to copywriting to ghostwriting, so that you can target the right opportunities for you.

Writing gigs come in many shapes and forms, including content creation, copywriting, ghostwriting, and more. Understanding the different opportunities available is essential for beginner writers looking to land their first gig.

Content creation covers a broad range of topics, from blog posts and articles to video scripts and audio podcasts. An aspiring writer can offer their services on freelance websites or contact potential clients directly. They can also reach out to companies or organizations with related interests that might benefit from content written by them. Creating high-quality pieces demonstrating the writer's knowledge and ability is paramount for success here.

Copywriting involves writing promotional material for businesses or other entities, such as ads, brochures, website landing pages, etc. If the composer's writing style fits what clients are looking for, they could be a great fit because, ideally, copywriters know how to make an impact with fewer words than other writing tasks require. It helps to have experience in advertising or marketing, but it isn't a must if the skill level is there.

Ghostwriting is another form of writing gig suitable for beginners trying to get their foot into the industry's door since it typically requires less experience than some other avenues. This type of work consists of writing content that will be attributed to someone else but still requires research and creativity—not only about the given topic but also about the voice of the intended recipient should bear in mind when crafting the piece.

No matter which field you decide to pursue as a beginning writer, understanding these opportunities can help guide your decision-making when selecting jobs that best suit your literary abilities. Researching client needs thoroughly before submitting samples can give you an edge when applying for freelance copywriting work.

4. Pitch yourself to potential clients through cold emails or job boards, offering specific examples of how your skills align with their needs.

Start by researching what skills the client is looking for, and highlight aspects that align with your expertise in your resume. If you don't have a formal background in writing but have qualifications in other sectors, emphasize how those abilities could help their business reach its goals.

Making connections with those involved in hiring decisions can also be beneficial. Creating a presence on social media outlets can increase your chances of getting noticed, as this opens up opportunities to communicate directly with employers regarding specific job postings.

In addition, don't forget that enthusiasm goes a long way. Showcase your creativity by engaging decision-makers through well-written messages tailored towards the position you are applying for that express why you feel you would be an ideal fit.

5. Communicate effectively and professionally throughout the hiring process and during projects, following guidelines and meeting deadlines as necessary.

As a freelance writer, one of the most important skills you can possess is effective communication. From the first inquiry to the final project delivery, clear and professional communication is critical to not only landing the gig but also securing future work with clients.

During the hiring process, it's essential to be timely and professional with your responses. Respond to inquiries and follow up with clients in a respectful and courteous manner. Listen actively to their needs and requirements, and provide relevant feedback and suggestions where appropriate. This will demonstrate your commitment to the project and your ability to work collaboratively with clients to achieve their goals.

Once the project is underway, continue to communicate effectively and professionally. This includes following guidelines and meeting deadlines as necessary. Be proactive in asking questions and clarifying requirements as needed to ensure that your work aligns with the client's needs.

Of course, sometimes unexpected issues arise that can impact project timelines. If this happens, it's crucial to communicate proactively with the client to discuss possible solutions and determine the best way forward. By demonstrating your flexibility and adaptability, you'll build trust and establish long-term relationships with your clients.

In your communication, maintain a professional, respectful tone. Avoid being confrontational or defensive, even if you disagree with the client's feedback or suggestions. Take time to thoughtfully consider feedback and suggestions and be willing to make changes as needed to ensure client satisfaction.

6. Determine your rates based on market research and the value of your work while also considering overhead expenses like self-employment taxes and insurance coverage.

Researching the market is essential when setting your rates as a freelance writer. Taking some time to understand what other freelancers are charging for similar services helps you determine a rate that's competitive and appropriate for your skillset and experience.

However, keep in mind that there are certain costs associated with running your own business that you need to consider when setting your rates. For instance, taxes for self-employed individuals can be higher than what employees pay, so plan accordingly. Additionally, make sure you have an emergency fund or an insurance policy in place that can cover any unexpected costs or health issues that arise during your career.

Finally, when establishing your rates as a freelancer, never forget the subjective value of your work. Stand by it and don't discount yourself – this industry is competitive enough without undercutting yourself. Put together an organized business plan and consider factors like location (if working remotely), overhead costs (time spent pitching vs actual writing) and more. All these things will help you figure out what rate works best for you and will maximize your earning potential as a professional writer.

7. Negotiate rates confidently, seeking fair compensation for both parties involved.

Negotiating rates is an essential part of any freelance writer's job, but it can be a challenge for many beginners. The key to successful negotiation is to approach it with confidence and a clear understanding of the value that you bring to the table.

When beginning negotiations, avoid feeling anxious or undervaluing your work by doing your research. Familiarize yourself with industry standards and rates, and take into account your experience and expertise. The goal is to arrive at a rate that is fair for both parties involved. Keep in mind that a client who is willing to pay for a high-quality service is more likely to be satisfied with the result, which is essential for future success.

During the negotiation process, it's crucial to communicate your value clearly and succinctly. This means being able to describe the benefits you offer, such as superior writing quality, professionalism, and the ability to meet deadlines consistently. This demonstrates that you take pride in your work and are dedicated to producing quality results, which sets you apart from other writers who may undersell their skills.

When negotiating with clients, always remain professional and respectful, even if the conversation becomes challenging at times. Listen carefully to their needs and concerns, and be willing to compromise if it aligns with your interests. By showing flexibility and open-mindedness, you can build trust with the client, which improves the likelihood of a long-term relationship.

8. Continually build upon your knowledge and skills by taking workshops or courses, reading literature within the field, and seeking feedback from peers.

As an aspiring freelance writer, there's always room for growth and improvement. One of the best ways to develop your skills and remain relevant is to invest in your professional development continually. This involves seeking out new knowledge and skills through workshops, courses, literature, and feedback from peers.

Attending workshops or courses relevant to your writing niche can introduce you to new techniques and best practices. You can learn effective ways of researching, marketing yourself, and improving your writing style. You can also expand your network and gain new professional contacts, which can lead to new writing opportunities and collaborations.

Reading literature within your field is another way to enhance your writing skills. You can keep up-to-date with new and emerging trends, technologies, and techniques. Reading a wide range of works also enhances your understanding of what makes compelling writing and empowers you to experiment with different writing styles.

Finally, seeking feedback from peers can be invaluable. Other writers can give you a different perspective on your work and identify areas where you can improve. By soliciting constructive criticism from people you trust, you'll be able to get a sense of your strengths and weaknesses as a writer and focus on what you can do to develop your skills.

9. Diversify your work by branching out into new industries or expanding your services to attract a

wider range of clients.

Another way to increase your chances of landing your first client is to diversify the work you offer. Consider branching out into new industries and offering services that may not have raised interest from clients previously.

For example, if you specialize in creating content for fashion magazines, look into writing content for health or lifestyle websites. You can also think outside the box and explore other types of writing, such as copywriting, scriptwriting, or news writing to reach a wider range of potential clients.

You can also expand the services you provide beyond just writing. Consider adding editing or proofreading services that can add value without creating brand-new content each time. Crafting a portfolio that showcases your ability to handle different assignments and genres will demonstrate the breadth of your creativity and talent and make it easier to compete against other writers in the field.

Diversifying your portfolio is an especially great strategy when starting out since it exposes you to different industries and experiences that help build your skillset and credibility with prospective employers. With a bit of effort you can easily expand on your existing talents, attracting more opportunities.

And finally...

10. Stay motivated by setting goals for yourself and celebrating each milestone along the way! With determination and these steps in mind, you'll be well on your way to growing a successful freelance writing career.

Reaching your goals as a freelance writer takes focus, determination, and dedication. The best way to stay motivated is to set clear, measurable, and achievable goals for yourself, both short-term and long-term. By setting a timeline for each goal and the steps you need to take to achieve it, you can easily keep track of your progress over time. Breaking down large goals into smaller steps makes them more manageable and gives you something tangible to work towards.

You should also remember that there will be times when things don't go according to plan. You may receive more rejections than assignments or simply feel stuck creatively. Learning how to manage these inevitable setbacks is key in developing resilience so that you can dust yourself off and get back on the path towards achieving your career goals faster than before.

Finally, don't forget to have fun. This isn't just about reaching milestones but also enjoying the journey by embracing new opportunities and experiences as a freelancer. When you stay motivated, determined, and focused on your objectives while having fun at the same time, there's no limit to what you can accomplish in growing a successful freelance writing career.

What To Do When You Find a Prospective Client

Receiving an inquiry from a prospective client can be exciting, but it can also be intimidating. As a freelance writer, you must ensure you're prepared to make the best impression and land the job. Here are some steps to take when responding to inquiries from prospective clients:

1. Show Your Appreciation & Interest

Acknowledge right away that you're happy they got in touch and let them know that their inquiry has your attention. This shows both appreciation and will help build trust between both parties.

Beginning freelance writers may overlook the importance of showing appreciation and interest in potential clients because they are eager to land their first gig and don't realize how much value it adds. New writers often underestimate the power of good communication skills and rush through their responses.

Additionally, due to inexperience, beginning writers may not understand that having a good rapport with their clients is essential for creating successful writing pieces. Without proper communication and appreciation, a new writer risks being passed over for future projects and losing out on potential income.

2. Ask Questions

Before accepting the assignment, make sure to ask any questions related to the project so that everyone involved is on the same page regarding expectations and deadlines. Find out what subtopics or angles are preferred and any other information relevant to the project.

Before agreeing to a freelance writing assignment, beginning freelancers need to ask the prospective client the following questions, such as:

- What is the overall goal of the project?
- Who will be the target audience?
- Are there any special formatting requirements or preferences?

- What type of timeline does the client expect?
- Is the client expecting any additional services such as research or editing?

Consider creating a questionnaire for new clients to streamline the onboarding process. An onboarding questionnaire is a valuable tool that freelance writers can use to set clear expectations with their clients and streamline the project management process. Here is an example of an onboarding questionnaire:

1. What is the scope of the project?
2. What is the goal of the project?
3. What is the deadline for the project?
4. What is the project budget?
5. Who is the target audience for the project?
6. What is the style or tone that you would like to convey in your content?
7. Is there any specific message or idea that you want to communicate through the project?
8. What types of content do you need? (e.g., blog posts, website copy, whitepapers, social media updates, etc.)
9. What is your preferred length for the content? (number of words or pages)
10. Do you have any examples of content that you'd like your project to emulate or be inspired by?
11. Are there any specific formatting requirements?
12. Do you have any resources that I should use or refer to while writing the content?
13. What is the process for submitting drafts, receiving feedback, and making revisions?
14. Will I be credited, and if so, how?
15. Is there anything else you'd like me to know about the project?

An onboarding questionnaire can help you clarify your client's needs and expectations, which can lead to more effective communication and reduce misunderstandings throughout the project.

3. Be Professional & Responsive

Always reply promptly so potential clients don't feel ignored — this is key in establishing yourself as an organized, reliable freelancer. When interacting with clients as a freelancer, it's crucial to create a professional and competent impression. Here are some best practices for sending professional emails to clients as a freelancer:

- Create a professional email address: Use an email address that is professional and relevant to your freelance work.
- Use a professional email signature: Include your name, business name, and relevant contact information, such as your phone number, email address, and social media profiles.
- Use a clear and concise subject line: The subject line should accurately summarize the purpose of the email in a few words. It should not be vague, misleading, or overly long.
- Address the client properly: Use the client's name and appropriate title while addressing them in the email. It's important to be respectful without being too casual.
- Be concise and organized: Keep the email content clear, concise, and well-organized. Avoid long paragraphs, irrelevant information, or extraneous details. Keep the email easy to read by using bullet points or numbered lists when needed.
- Check for errors: Always proofread your email before sending it. Check for spelling, grammar, and punctuation errors. It's important to present yourself as professional and competent.
- Follow up: Keep in touch with clients throughout the project

and after project delivery. This helps to build a good relationship and ensures customer satisfaction.
- Use a friendly but professional tone: Your tone should provide a friendly and approachable feel without being too informal or casual.
- Use the appropriate level of formality: Gauge the client's communication style and match it for your email. Some clients prefer formality, while others may be more relaxed.

By following these best practices for sending emails to clients as a freelancer, you'll be able to present yourself as a professional and competent writer. This will improve your chances of landing new clients (and retaining old ones).

4. Share Relevant Samples

Having a portfolio of writing samples at hand shows off your skill set without needing words. Most projects need different styles of writing, so having content ready for presentation can be very helpful. If available, make sure to share pieces of work related to the project being proposed.

One of the best ways for freelance writers to show a prospective client samples of their work is to create an online portfolio or website that showcases their writing. This is a great way to demonstrate the writer's skills and professionalism and give the potential client an easy way to view examples of previously completed projects.

Additionally, freelance writers can use services such as LinkedIn and other professional networking sites to share their published works with others in the industry. Writers can also reach out directly via email and provide links to select samples of their writing when responding to inquiries from potential clients.

5. Negotiate Rates & Deadlines

Quoting too low or too high of a price for a freelance writing project is risky, as it can lead to either missing out on necessary compensation or a negative impression from the prospective client. Similarly, overpromising and underdelivering can also be detrimental. If the freelancer is consistently late in delivering quality work or sets unrealistic deadlines, this can create strained relationships with clients, impacting future business opportunities.

To reduce this risk, it is important to be reasonable and transparent when negotiating rates and deadlines by factoring in all associated costs and setting realistic expectations for delivery. Negotiating rates and deadlines with clients is often challenging, especially for beginner freelancers. Here are some best practices for negotiating rates and deadlines effectively:

- Research: Before negotiating rates and deadlines, research industry standards and going rates for the type of work you'll be doing. This will give you a good idea of the market value of your work, and you'll be able to set competitive prices accordingly.
- Be confident: Come to the negotiation process with confidence in your abilities and the value that you bring to the project. Remember that you're an expert in your field, and you deserve to be fairly compensated for your work.
- Set clear expectations: Clearly define the scope of the project, the deadline and the budget with the client in the negotiation process so that everyone is on the same page.
- Prioritize mutual benefit: While you want to be compensated fairly for your work, it's important to prioritize a mutually beneficial outcome for both you and your client.
- Determine your target rate: Have a clear idea of your target

rate in mind that is based on your research and takes into account your experience and expertise.
- Be Flexible: Be willing to negotiate and make compromises as necessary. Don't be too stubborn and always keep an open mind.
- Present evidence: When presenting your rate to a client, present data or proof behind the amount so that they can see the reasoning behind it.
- Offer payment options: With payment options, clients feel they can choose their payment schedule and won't feel as though the expenses are a shock.
- Be respectful: Always maintain a respectful and professional demeanor when negotiating rates and deadlines.

55 Writing Gigs for Freelancers

Landing a writing gig can be an exciting yet challenging journey for aspiring writers. With so many different types of writing to explore and endless possibilities at your fingertips, it can be hard to decide which direction to take. Writing gigs offer a great opportunity to turn your passion into a career, but with such a wide selection of genres and formats, it can be difficult to know where to start.

The key is to trust your instincts and follow your gut. The right gig will eventually reveal itself if you remain open to trying new things. Whether you're looking to break into the world of copywriting or aim higher by attempting screenplays and documentaries, plenty of options are just waiting for you to explore them.

From blogging and product descriptions all the way up to short stories and novels, here's a list of 55 different writing gigs you could get involved in today, listed in alphabetic order:

1. Ad copy
2. Affiliate marketing
3. Articles
4. Blog posts
5. Case studies
6. Competitive analysis
7. Consulting on a freelance basis
8. Copyediting
9. Creating an online course
10. Creating or updating a style guide
11. Ebooks
12. E-learning modules
13. Email newsletters
14. Facilitating copywriting workshops
15. Forming a strategic partnership with another business
16. Ghostwriting
17. Grant writing
18. How-to guides
19. Instructional design
20. Interview questions
21. Joining or starting an agency
22. Landing pages
23. LinkedIn profiles
24. Managing other freelance writers
25. Market research
26. Messaging and positioning documents
27. Naming projects
28. Photo captions
29. Podcast episodes
30. Powerful headlines
31. PowerPoint presentations
32. Presenting at conferences or meetups

33. Press releases
34. Product descriptions
35. Proofreading
36. Publishing a book
37. Reports
38. Resumes and cover letters
39. Sales letters
40. Scripts for webinars and webcasts
41. Social media content
42. Song lyrics
43. Speeches
44. Starting your own freelance writing business
45. Survey analysis and interpretation
46. Survey questions
47. Taglines and slogans
48. Theatre and movie reviews
49. Transcriptions
50. User manuals
51. Video scripts
52. Web content rewriting
53. Web copy
54. White papers
55. Working as part of an in-house marketing team

No matter what type of writing suits your interests and expertise best, there are ample opportunities to express yourself as a freelance writer. So take the time to explore which type of work is best for you and start making your mark as a content creator!

Chapter 6 Should You Work With an Agency or Go Directly to the Client?

As an experienced freelance writer, I know all too well the challenges that come with working with both agencies and directly with clients. Through my own experience, I've found that when it comes to agencies, it can be beneficial to work with them as they generally have access to larger pools of potential clients and offer services beyond content creation such as SEO optimization or a suite of marketing services.

However, it's important to note that these companies often reduce the rates of the freelancers in order for them to increase the fees they charge their clients. Working directly with the client can provide more control over your income rate but also presents its own set of challenges that should be considered.

Working With an Agency

Working with an agency can be a great way for new freelance writers to gain experience and establish contact with potential clients. Agencies often have their own network of connections not available to the general public, so freelancers have access to more opportunities than they could find on their own. Furthermore, agencies handle all the paperwork and financial details, so freelancers don't have to worry about dealing with contracts or tax issues.

Agencies also provide better job security than going it alone since writers have a consistent source of income from the agency instead of continually looking for new clients. By providing new writers with support and a platform for growth, agencies make sure that freelance writers get the most out of their projects and increase their chances for success in the long run.

Pros and Cons of Working With an Agency

For freelance writers, working with an agency can be a great way to increase the number of potential clients and gain experience. However, it's important to consider both the positives and negatives of such an arrangement before signing any contracts. I've compiled a list of 10 advantages and 10 drawbacks that every freelancer should consider when deciding whether to work with an agency.

Advantages of Working with an Agency

1. Access to a larger network of potential clients.

2. Faster job application process and easier vetting.

3. Additional services such as marketing and legal support.

4. Takes care of tax reporting and invoices, reducing the bureaucratic burden on freelancers.

5. Consistent source of income.

6. Easier access to experienced professionals.

7. Guidance and mentorship from agency staff.

8. Increase in the number of available opportunities.

9. Professional collaboration environment to share resources and skills.

10. Opportunity for career growth through the agency's network.

Drawbacks of Working with an Agency

1. Lack of control over work assignments or projects.

2. Reduced ability to set your own rates/fees.

3. Limited exposure to potential long-term customers or relationships beyond the agency contract.

4. Loss of independence as you are bound by the agency's rules and regulations.

5. Restrictions on client communication, leading to delays in obtaining project feedback or input from end-users.

6. Increased competition among freelance writers for jobs & projects.

7. Potentially lower earnings due to fees & commissions charged by the agency.

8. Unclear expectations from the agency can lead to misunderstandings and disagreements.

9. Financial risks if an agreement between an agency and client is canceled.

10. Rigid timelines that may not match up with individual needs.

Best Practices for Finding an Agency To Write For

When looking for an agency to write for, it is important to do your research and focus on finding the right fit. You will want to find an agency with experience in the areas you are interested in, a positive reputation, and good working relationships with their writing staff.

To begin your search, reach out to writers or editors you know personally who have had success with agencies. Ask if they can provide recommendations or insight into their experiences. Additionally, consider utilizing online resources such as directories and portals that list verified and reputable agencies. Take some time to read through reviews from former clients and research any policies around payment terms and contracts.

Once you've found a few potential agencies that seem like a good fit for what you're looking for, schedule a meeting (virtually if necessary) to discuss your expectations, pricing structure, workloads, the types of projects available, turnaround times and any other relevant information. Consider all potential risks during your interview, such as working under non-disclosure agreements or intellectual property rights issues.

Finally, when deciding whether or not an agency is right for you, consider factors such as strong communication lines between yourself and the agency's team members and the level of support you feel comfortable having when tackling projects. It is ultimately up to each freelancer to decide whether or not working with an agency is right for them—but hopefully these suggestions can help make this decision easier.

Working Directly With a Client

Working directly with clients as a freelance writer has its advantages. First and foremost, it gives you greater control over the type of work you do, which can help you build a portfolio and establish yourself as an expert in your niche. When you work directly with a client, you have the opportunity to build a relationship with them, which can lead to repeat business and referrals.

Another benefit of working directly with a client is that you can set your own rates. Although negotiating rates can be challenging, it allows you to charge what you feel you are worth and avoid the commission fees that some agencies charge. In addition, since you'll have more control over the projects you work on, you'll also have more control over your schedule and work hours.

While these advantages may seem appealing, working directly with clients also has its challenges. Since you are responsible for finding your own clients and projects, there may be times when work is scarce. Additionally, managing clients and handling administrative tasks can be time-consuming, taking valuable time away from your writing.

Pros and Cons of Working With a Client Directly

For many freelance writers, working directly with a client instead of an agency is an attractive option due to its potential for increased earnings, career development opportunities and closer ties with the client. But certain drawbacks need to be considered before taking this path. Here are 10 advantages and 10 drawbacks of working directly with clients as a freelance writer.

Advantages of Working Directly With a Client

1. Can negotiate a higher rate for projects.

2. Have the opportunity to develop a strong relationship with the client.

3. Greater control over project details and outcomes.

4. Be able to showcase specific specialist knowledge correctly and in detail.

5. No need to compete with other writers within an agency.

6. Closer ties with the client enable real-time feedback and guidance throughout the process.

7. Easier to manage expectations as both parties are aware of each other's needs.

8. Allows more flexible opportunities for choosing which project to work on.

9. Improved career development opportunities by understanding clients' individual needs and preferences.

10. Potential for long-term relationships that benefit both parties.

Drawbacks to Working Directly With a Client

1. More responsibility for managing all aspects of the projects, including communication, payment, and dispute resolution.

2. Could take longer for payments if working directly with a client instead of an agency.

3. Increased nonpayment or late payment risk without an agency acting as an intermediary between freelancer and client.

4. Less access to regular gigs or job opportunities since assignments may not be consistent.

5. Risk of upfront work requirements from some clients before making payment.

6. Difficulty staying organized when dealing with multiple clients instead of one agency.

7. Complexity in maintaining taxes when dealing with revenue from multiple clients.

8. Need to build up trust with each client before they hire you again.

9. Lack of protection if things go wrong during a project.

10. Need more time spent on marketing yourself and finding new clients.

Agencies or Clients: Which Is Right for You?

When it comes to making a decision between working with an agency or clients directly as a freelancer, there are several factors that need to be considered to help you make an informed decision. It's important to weigh the pros and cons of each approach, and understand what aligns with your career goals.

To help you decide which approach is right for you, here are some questions to consider:

1. What are your strengths and weaknesses?

Assessing your skills, abilities, and areas of expertise can help you determine which approach is best suited for you. If you have a deep knowledge of a particular industry or niche, working directly with clients in that space can help you establish yourself as an expert. On the other hand, if you don't enjoy handling administrative tasks or prefer flexibility, working with an agency might be better suited for you.

2. What kind of work do you want to do?

If you're interested in a specific type of writing or want to have more control over the projects you work on, working directly with clients may be the best approach. However, if you're looking for a steady flow of work and opportunities to learn new skills, an agency may be a better fit.

3. How important is financial stability to you?

Agencies can offer stable work and regular paychecks, but the cost is that they may take a commission from your rate. Working directly with clients can provide higher rates, but not stability. Decide on your priorities.

4. What's important to you in your career?

Different writers have different and unique goals. If you value long-term relationships with clients, working directly might offer you with repeat business and referrals. If you want growth and experience several clients within different industries, agencies would be a perfect fit.

When it comes down to it, there isn't a wrong or right option, as both approaches have their advantages and their disadvantages. Successful freelances tend to work both with clients directly and via agencies. It depends on the available opportunities presented to you and what corresponds best with your priorities and goals.

Chapter 7 How To Find High-Paying Writing Jobs and Clients

As a freelance writer, I remember the days when I was scraping by, living paycheck to paycheck, and worrying about whether I'd be able to make rent each month. But all of that changed when I began putting in the work to build my freelance business, and started generating steady income.

As my income began to grow, I felt a sense of relief that I had never experienced before. No longer did I need to worry about whether I'd have enough money to make ends meet. Instead, I could focus on doing work that I truly enjoyed and was passionate about, without the constant financial stress.

But it wasn't until I hit the six-figure mark that I truly realized how far I had come. Knowing that my hard work had paid off and that I was able to earn a substantial income as a self-employed writer was a feeling unlike any other.

Being able to pay all of my bills, including my housing costs, was incredibly empowering. It gave me a sense of control over my finances that I had never experienced before. And it allowed me to reinvest in myself and my business, taking on new and exciting projects that I may not have been able to afford otherwise.

If you're an aspiring freelance writer or content creator, I want to tell you that it is possible to reach this level of success. It takes time, dedication, and a willingness to put in the work, but the rewards are more than worth it. So keep pushing yourself, keep honing your craft, and before you know it, you too could be generating a six-figure income doing what you love.

In this chapter, we will look at the basics of how to go about finding higher-paying writing jobs and clients, what expectations you should have in terms of pay rates, how experience is key when seeking out great clients, as well as tips on relevant niches and resources to utilize.

How Much Can You Earn as a Freelance Writer?

Earning $100K or more as a freelance writer is definitely a realistic goal, but it requires dedication and discipline. Various strategies can help you optimize your earning potential, such as setting up fair pricing structures and offering related services that require little additional work to earn extra income.

When it comes to pricing strategies for freelance writers, it's important to be realistic when quoting rates. You should consider the project's scope, the amount of research and writing required, and any other services or resources you may need to provide to complete the job - such as design work, illustrations or photography - and account for all these factors in your quote.

Freelancers who bill hourly gain a degree of autonomy that other workers don't necessarily have, as they are free to establish their own policies concerning when and how payment is due. In addition, if you can take on recurring clients who need regular services from you on an ongoing basis - such as website content management or blog writing - charging a flat per-article or monthly rate can significantly increase your earnings potential.

Another great way for freelance writers to increase their income is to offer related services that require little extra effort. This could include proofreading work for existing clients or editing posts for other blogs or websites. Other options include researching and curating content-related topics for clients, helping them develop marketing plans and creating professional-quality infographics or presentations based on written content they create. By taking advantage of these opportunities and offering them through your freelance writing services, you can easily expand your source of income beyond just writing alone.

Remember that quality should always come before quantity in freelance writing if you want to make more net income. Yes, taking on more projects may result in higher *gross* income, but the quality of each project should not be compromised to hit those earnings goals. If writing clients are not satisfied with your work due to poor quality and care, they will quickly move on to other options. If this happens, client turnover can greatly reduce your earning potential if you find yourself having to look for new clients or projects frequently.

Putting quality first also means you can charge more per project and attract higher-paying clients and repeat customers who know they're always getting reliable and exceptional work. Additionally, word-of-mouth can help build your reputation as a freelance writer, exposing more potential clients to your services who are willing to pay premium rates. It's important to remember that although it may initially take longer to establish yourself as a high-quality freelancer, it can result in long-term financial success if you stick with it.

Having the Right Expectations in Terms of Pay Rates and Client Requirements

As a freelance writer, it's important to understand the necessary components for correctly setting your pay rate and meeting client expectations. There are several essential elements to remember when arriving at these decisions.

Firstly, it is important to be aware of the type of clients who may be willing to pay more for your services. Typically, larger companies or corporate entities will want to hire experienced and qualified freelancers for higher rates. As such, it is worth networking and building contacts within these spheres to access these opportunities. Additionally, suppose you specialize in a particular sub-niche or can provide a specific service that large businesses or organizations need. In that case, you may have an easier time seeking higher-paying projects.

For example, if you specialize in writing technical content for software companies, you may be able to charge a premium for your expertise because there are fewer writers with that specific knowledge. Similarly, if you're an expert in SEO writing, you may be able to command a higher rate because your skills are in high demand.

If you're a content creator, specializing in a specific type of content can also help you earn higher-paying projects. For example, if you're a social media marketer who specializes in creating video content for Facebook and Instagram, you may be able to charge more for your services because video content is a highly sought-after skill.

Another example would be freelance writers who specialize in case studies for particular industries such as healthcare or finance. These writers often charge premium rates because they have extensive knowledge of the industry and can provide valuable insights and data in their content.

Keeping track of industry trends can also help position yourself in the market when negotiating prices. With this increased knowledge of what certain specializations command in the current market and an understanding of the value you offer to clients, you should be able to strike deals that perfectly balance their needs with your desired rate per project. It's important not to undervalue yourself and your services, so make sure that any pay rate should at least reflect the market standards - if not exceed them.

For projects with demanding client requirements that could quickly eat into your hourly rate or budgeted project prices, remember it often pays to think of long-term return on investment (ROI) rather than just one deal. Keeping your target audience's needs in mind and considering how this project could bring both immediate profit but also valuable future connections/business relationships is key here – both financially and professionally. Balancing client requirements with realistic payment structures can be incredibly profitable in the long run if managed properly.

Gaining Relevant Experience To Increase Your Chances of Finding Higher-Paying Clients

Building up your portfolio and becoming an expert in the field will always be beneficial when accessing better projects and opportunities. Taking on small, low-paying jobs can also help boost your writing experience and give you the confidence to take on more complex or higher-budgeted tasks. Additionally, networking with other professionals in the industry can open up doors you may never have thought possible.

It's also important to remember that building a solid reputation is key. This goes beyond just securing great reviews from your clients. It's also about consistently delivering quality work over time while staying true to yourself and maintaining your unique style. This is what will truly set you apart from the competition and make sure that potential employers recognize you as someone who reliably produces exceptional results every single time.

Finally, always stay flexible regarding payment terms, as this shows employers that you are willing to tailor a project around their needs without compromising quality or delivery timescales. Doing so shows them that you understand their requirements and are willing to go above and beyond for them at an agreeable rate. Clients appreciate this level of dedication and reliability, which is often rewarded with requests for future projects.

Searching for Niches to Specialize In That Have the Potential for Higher Earnings

Choosing the right niche for your freelance writing career can be challenging, but it's also important to remember that finding high-paying niches and sub-niches is often the key to success. A niche is a specialized field of expertise, and sub-niches are smaller segments within that category. Finding these niches that pay well can be done by researching the market and staying on top of industry trends to identify areas with higher demand than usual.

When searching for high-paying niches, one of the best practices is using online resources such as job boards that list current openings in the writing sphere. Doing so will allow you to get an idea of what companies are looking for and how much they're willing to pay for specific services. Additionally, building connections with industry professionals and establishing yourself as someone reliable within certain fields could lead to more opportunities opening up down the line.

Some examples of high-earning niches or sub-niches include:

- Technical writing (especially for software and technology companies)
- SEO writing (including keyword research and optimization)
- Social media marketing (including creating and managing paid ad campaigns)
- Content marketing (including email marketing and lead generation)

- Copywriting (especially for e-commerce websites and sales funnels)
- Case studies (for various industries such as healthcare and finance)
- Whitepapers and research reports (for academic or business purposes)
- Grant writing (for non-profit organizations and government agencies)
- Product reviews (especially for tech and lifestyle products)
- Ghostwriting (for books, speeches, and articles)
- Scriptwriting (for film and television)
- Travel writing (especially for luxury destinations)
- Food and beverage writing (including restaurant reviews and cookbooks)
- Health and wellness writing (including natural remedies and nutrition)

Generally speaking, any field where businesses are highly invested in their communications strategies tend to require higher quality content which often pays far more than the average writer rate, making them prime targets when exploring potential areas of specialization.

It's important to note that while these niches and sub-niches have the potential to earn higher rates, it's also important for freelance writers and content creators to have a genuine interest and expertise in the subject matter. Working in a niche that you are passionate about can make the work more enjoyable and rewarding.

Building Up Your Profile and Network for Better Opportunities With High-Paying Clients

Building up your profile and network as a freelance writer is essential to improving your chances of securing better opportunities with high-paying clients. Every client you work with should come with the opportunity to leave a positive impression and establish yourself as a reliable and valued professional in their eyes. This is achieved by ensuring your work meets expectations, delivering on time, communicating effectively, and maintaining regular contact if needed.

Networking is also an important part of this process. It's not just about making connections but also staying active within circles that provide relevant information on new job openings or industry trends. Joining targeted communities such as Facebook groups, local freelance guilds, or specialized conferences are all excellent ways to stay abreast of the market and join conversations with those with similar interests or goals. Additionally, it's important to remember that networking comes in many forms – from casual email exchanges, exchanging knowledge through blog posts or podcasts, and even attending online webinars hosted by experts in the field. All these things can help build up your profile while providing additional leads for potential jobs.

Finally, don't forget the power of referrals. If you've done great work for a client in the past, they may be more than happy to refer you when an opportunity comes knocking, potentially leading to higher paychecks for future projects. The key takeaway is that maintaining strong relationships in this industry pays off.

Asking for Client Referrals

Asking for a client referral is an important part of the freelance writer's journey. However, it should be done appropriately and professionally to maximize the likelihood of success.

The first step is to make sure you have established yourself as a reliable and reputable professional in your client's eyes. Make sure that all the work you do for them has been completed on time and with high quality so that they will be more inclined to vouch for you when asked.

Additionally, maintain consistent contact with your client - this could involve sending them periodic updates on how their project is progressing or checking in periodically even after completing the job to stay connected. This will demonstrate your commitment to their success and show you are dedicated to providing excellent customer service each time.

Next, when asking for a referral from a client or colleague, it's important to avoid making it appear like it's just about making more money. This can come across as insincere and may make it less likely for the person to want to refer you to others. So how can you ask for a referral in a way that benefits both parties? Here's an example:

Dear [Client/Colleague],

I wanted to reach out and say thank you for the opportunity to work with you on [previous project]. I enjoyed collaborating with you and am happy to hear that you were pleased with the end result.

As you know, I'm a freelance writer/content creator, and I'm always looking to expand my network and take on new projects. I was wondering if you know anyone who might be in need of content creation services, particularly in [your specialized sub-niche].

If you have any connections or colleagues who could benefit from my services, I'd be grateful if you could pass my name along. I would also be happy to provide a referral for you if you're ever in need of [service/product].

Thanks again for your time, and I look forward to the possibility of working with you again in the future.

Best regards, [Your Name]

In this example, the focus is on expressing gratitude for the past collaboration and on building a relationship for future collaboration. By mentioning your specialized sub-niche, you're providing a clear idea of the type of work you do and who would benefit from your services. Additionally, by offering to be a referral for the client or colleague, you're demonstrating that this is not just a one-sided request for more business, but rather a way to benefit both parties through collaboration and mutual support.

Finally, provide any necessary re-assurances that may help incentivize them, such as showcasing samples of your previous work for the client or guaranteeing additional discounts or loyalty rewards if they refer someone else who ends up signing with you. Keep communication channels open, and make sure your clients know how much you value their input. By doing so, referrals can become mutually beneficial opportunities moving forward.

Developing Effective Strategies To Help You Find Clients Who Pay Well

The ability to find high-paying clients is a key factor in the success of any freelance writer. However, you must be able to differentiate yourself from the competition and offer something unique. Developing effective strategies can help you stand out and make it easier for potential clients to see why hiring you as a freelancer benefits them.

Here are 9 strategies that any freelancer can follow to find higher-paying clients:

1. Create a portfolio website: Your website should contain strong, relevant samples of your work that showcase your skills and professionalism. Make sure that it reflects who you are and the type of projects you're best suited for so that potential customers know exactly what they're getting when they hire you.

2. Research industry trends: Knowing what's "hot" in the market right now can help guide your search for better-paying jobs and give you ideas on differentiating yourself from other applicants with similar qualifications.

3. Reach out through social media: Use social media sites to reach out to prospective clients, and make sure you include links back to your own portfolio site whenever possible.

4. Take advantage of professional networking platforms: Professional networks such as LinkedIn and the Upwork Freelancer Community are excellent for connecting with other professionals in related fields and providing job referrals. Taking part in industry forums or groups may also prove valuable here –as long as everyone involved takes time to stay active.

5. Reply directly on job postings: Look out for specific job postings that look promising and send off personalized applications tailored towards them instead of generic inquiries. To personalize an application, tailor your message and qualifications to the job posting, highlighting relevant skills and experience.

6. Ask for referrals from past or current clients: If you have had a successful project or working relationship with someone previously, don't be afraid to ask them if they know anyone else who might be looking for writers at their level. This could potentially lead to new opportunities with better pay.

7. Track down editors at major publications: Editors at major publications often have contacts in various industries who may be looking for freelance writers. So, do some research into who they are and shoot them an email asking how best to get in touch so that you can pitch ideas accordingly.

8. Consider joining exclusive membership sites: Some allow access only upon invitation, so look into these if traditional methods haven't yielded results. Access will enable you to view highly sought-after gigs which also offer great payment packages.

9. Offer a free consultation: Offering a free consultation can help establish a relationship with potential clients and demonstrate your expertise. It can also increase the likelihood of landing higher-paid projects.

Resources That Help Freelancers Find High-Paying Writing Jobs

As a freelancer, finding high-paying writing jobs can often seem impossible. However, with the right resources and platforms available to writers, such as Upwork, Medium and others, finding those lucrative projects often isn't as challenging as it might seem.

Upwork is arguably one of the most popular go-to sites for freelance professionals seeking high-paying writing jobs. With their vast network of employers worldwide offering job postings ranging from copywriting to content creation, it's fairly easy to land a client on the platform if you have the needed skills. Aside from providing an effective way to connect with potential clients, Upwork also offers additional tools such as project management and time tracking that enable freelancers to manage their projects more efficiently.

In addition to Upwork, there are other platforms for writers who may want to explore different opportunities or try something new. Medium is a great platform for writers to showcase their skills, build an audience and increase their visibility in the industry. By creating and sharing quality content, writers can gain a following of other writers and potential clients who may be interested in hiring them for high-paying writing jobs. Furthermore, through networking with other writers on

Medium, freelance professionals can also find useful referrals which could open up even more opportunities for lucrative gigs.

Finally, various other resources are also available online, depending on what type of writing you're looking for. Some of these include the ProBlogger Job Board, which helps bloggers connect with companies seeking blog post writers. LinkedIn ProFinder similarly allows professionals in any field (including writing) to connect with potential employers. All these resources provide valuable insight into the freelance market and could potentially lead you toward projects that pay well.

Why Relying on a Single Source of Business is Risky for Freelance Content Creators

Freelance content creators who rely solely on a single source or method for getting business are setting themselves up for potential failure. While it's great to have a reliable and consistent source of income, by putting all your eggs in one basket, you're limiting your opportunities for growth and success. Additionally, relying on one source or method can leave you vulnerable to changes in the market, shifts in demand, and unforeseen circumstances such as a client budget cuts.

Effective prospecting is all about casting a wide net and using multiple approaches to attract potential clients. This isn't just a good idea – it's essential to staying relevant, building a strong client base, and positioning yourself for continued success.

One of the key benefits of using several approaches to prospecting is that it allows you to identify the methods that work best for you and your business. While one method may work well for one writer, it may not work as effectively for another. By experimenting with different approaches, you can discover the ones that are most efficient and effective for your business, and leverage them to maximize your success.

Additionally, consistent prospecting is crucial to continued growth and success in the industry. Even if you have a full schedule of clients booked, it's important to keep prospecting for new business to ensure a steady stream of work in the future. By consistently reaching out to potential clients and casting a wide net, you're increasing your chances of landing high-quality clients and expanding your network.

Moreover, having multiple sources of business helps you maintain your independence as a freelancer. By building a diversified portfolio, you have more control over your income and career trajectory. You can be more selective about the projects you take on, and not be forced to take on low-paying or unenjoyable projects simply because you need the income.

In conclusion, for freelance content creators, using multiple approaches to prospecting is key to building a successful and sustainable business. By casting a wide net, experimenting with different methods, and maintaining consistent prospecting efforts, you can expand your network, build a diversified portfolio, and ensure your continued growth and success in the industry.

Chapter 8 Fighting Lowball Offers and Negotiating Better Rates for Your Writing

As a freelance writer, I've experienced my fair share of lowball offers. It's frustrating to put time and effort into crafting high-quality content, only to have clients who don't understand the true value of our work and expect us to work for peanuts. But the truth is, lowball offers are an unfortunate reality in the world of freelance writing, and it's up to us to learn how to deal with them effectively.

One of the main reasons why clients may offer low rates is because they simply don't understand the value of the work that we do. They may not realize that quality content takes time and effort to create or that it has the potential to drive traffic and increase engagement. Instead, they may view content creation as a simple task that anyone can do, and therefore, they are unwilling to pay a premium for it.

Another reason why clients may offer low rates is that they are trying to keep their costs down. In a competitive market, many clients may be looking for ways to save money, and offering low rates to writers is one way to do that. Unfortunately, this can lead to a race to the bottom, with clients seeking out the cheapest writers possible rather than those who offer the best quality work.

So what can you do as a freelance writer to combat lowball offers? The key is to educate clients about the value of your work and to negotiate for better rates. In the following chapter, we'll explore some effective strategies for negotiating better rates, including how to identify your worth as a writer, how to frame your value proposition to clients, and how to build relationships with clients that will make them more willing to pay for quality work. By learning these key techniques, you'll be better equipped to stand up for yourself as a writer and fight for fair compensation for your valuable work.

Researching Market Rates for Freelance Writing Services

Researching the market rate for freelance writing services is important in setting your rate and ensuring you receive fair compensation. It's essential to thoroughly understand the industry standards and know what other writers charge for similar projects.

Here are some best practices when it comes to researching market rates:

1. Network with Other Freelance Writers – Connect with other writers in your field and ask them questions about their rates or experiences negotiating better rates from clients.

2. Check Professional Associations – See what freelance writing associations have published, such as rate surveys or information about prevailing wages for different writing services.

3. Perform Online Research – Conduct online searches to find out what other writers are earning in your niche area and look at job postings that mention payment amounts.

4. Utilize Freelance Writing Job Boards – Check job boards like Upwork or ProBlogger regularly by searching terms related to your specialty to get a sense of what companies are offering for similar services outside your local area or country.

5. Leverage Social Media Platforms – Look through social media groups dedicated to freelance writing and join conversations about current market rates for specific jobs or areas of expertise you may be interested in pursuing further down the line.

Understanding the Value of Your Work and Setting Your Rate Accordingly

When setting a rate as a freelance writer, understanding the value of your work to the client is essential. It's important to take the time to determine how much you are worth and to be confident in the rate that you set for yourself. After all, if you don't think you deserve it, why should a client?

Understanding your value starts with research. Research what experienced writers in the same field are charging for similar services. Consider all of your qualifications, experience and skill level when determining how much you should charge for your work. Additionally, look at other factors such as market demands, client expectations and current economic trends – these can all affect the rate you set.

Once you feel comfortable with the rate that works for both you and your clients, stick to it. You may encounter some clients who will balk at this rate due to budgeting issues, or they may try and lowball you by offering less than your asking price. When faced with this dilemma, be firm yet polite in asserting the value of your work while still respecting their budget constraints. Don't let yourself get pushed around. Make sure that any negotiations reflect a mutual understanding of what each party expects from their agreement and ultimately aim to benefit both sides fairly.

Ultimately, valuing one's work is about recognizing our worth and committing to advocating for ourselves professionally within an often competitive industry. Accurately pricing freelance writing services requires considering multiple factors across various industries while also keeping abreast of changes in the field which could alter our rates over time. But by properly researching market rates, understanding our value, and confidently setting our rates accordingly, we can ensure a successful career as freelancers where we can receive the fair compensation we deserve for our hard work.

How To Respond to a Lowball Offer Without Losing Out on Potential Work

When freelancing, it's not uncommon to be met with a lowball offer. This can be incredibly discouraging and leave you feeling taken advantage of for your hard work in prospecting for clients. However, there are ways to respond to potential clients that make clear that your skills and services are valued while still leaving the door open for future opportunities.

The first step is to remain professional in your response. Express your understanding of their budget constraints while also expressing dismay at their lowball offer. Make sure they know that while you respect their budgetary limitations, you must also value your work and ask for an appropriate fee to reflect this value. Explain why now isn't the right time for discounted pricing – don't just say no – explain why this isn't feasible, so they understand where you're coming from.

If possible, include suggestions for alternative solutions or services you could provide within their specified budget. Offer flexible payment plans if needed or propose working on smaller parts of the overall project in increments to fit within the client's parameters.

Additionally, suggest other options such as referrals or trade-offs. If a client truly values your work and it fits into their budget constraints, then consider offering lower-priced services in exchange for referrals. This way, you may receive a more consistent income flow without sacrificing equity in the long run.

Finally, consider if a lower price point is feasible after all. Freelancers need a balance between earning enough money to sustain themselves while also remaining competitive amongst other professionals in their field. With some creative negotiation, finding that sweet spot while still providing valuable services at an appropriate rate may be possible.

Strategies for Negotiating a Higher Rate With Clients

The first step for negotiating a higher rate is research. Look into what experienced writers in the same field charge for similar services. Consider all of your qualifications, experience and skill level when determining how much to ask for. This should form the starting point for negotiations. Additionally, look at other factors such as market demand, client expectations and current economic trends – these can all affect the rate you set and provide additional value when proposing a fee increase.

Second, know your worth. This involves researching industry standards and professional rates for freelancers and feeling confident enough to stand behind those numbers during negotiations with potential clients. If you don't believe in yourself and your value, then why should they? Be sure to explain why you are worth more than your competitor and provide evidence, such as feedback from past clients or successful projects as proof of others seeing value in your work.

Don't be afraid to walk away if an offer isn't satisfactory. Sometimes saying no can pave the way toward a better outcome by clarifying that you understand your worth and won't settle for less than it deserves. Finally, consider alternative negotiation methods such as offering flexible payment plans or exchanging lower-priced services in exchange for referrals; both can help achieve better rates without sacrificing quality or equity in the long run.

Different Ways To Proactively Increase Your

Income as a Freelancer

As a freelance copywriter, it is essential to continuously look for ways to proactively increase your income and stay competitive in the freelancing market instead of waiting for business to come to you. Copywriters can explore many creative ways to make extra money and increase their overall earnings.

Take advantage of opportunities offered by clients. Don't be afraid to ask for a higher rate if it reflects the value of your work or even suggest other services you can provide, such as SEO, graphic design, editing, or social media engagement. Make sure you are pitching more than just what was asked of you, and impress clients with other things you can offer. Networking is also a great way to expand your reach.

Another great way to increase your income is by upselling existing clients on more expensive packages that include different services like website content creation, stock images or monthly newsletters. You should also consider creating packages based around recurring maintenance services such as blog writing or weekly emails. Doing so is an easy way to secure reliable income over several months instead of just one-time payments.

Finally, some freelance copywriters have been able to create content for books and courses, which can be profitable in the long run. Writing short e-books or creating online courses are excellent ways to generate passive income that requires minimal effort from then on out.

Here are a few different ways a freelance copywriter could increase their income:

- Offering SEO services.
- Writing short e-books.
- Creating recurring content maintenance services.

- Offering graphic design services.
- Providing social media engagement services.
- Editing content for other freelancers or companies.
- Creating content for books and courses.
- Writing monthly newsletters.
- Offering copywriting services for unique platforms, such as Medium and Substack.
- Creating an online store to sell copies of your writing.
- Developing corporate writing training courses.
- Creating and selling specialized freelance writing templates.
- Ghostwriting articles for other authors or companies.

Sub-Contracting Your Way to Incremental Income

So what happens if you cannot personally provide some of these services? That's where sub-contracting comes in. Sub-contracting is a great option for freelancers who cannot provide certain services themselves or have too much on their plate. Sub-contracting allows you to outsource your workload by hiring other professionals to manage specific tasks and projects.

This can help you incrementally increase your income by allowing you to take on more projects and charge higher rates when necessary. However, it's important to consider both the pros and cons before adding a sub-contractor to your team.

Pros of sub-contracting:

- You can focus on tasks more suitable for your skillset instead of wasting time trying to figure out how to do something unfamiliar.
- You can easily scale up and tackle larger projects that would

otherwise be difficult to handle alone.
- You can access talents from all over the world, often at a more affordable rate than hiring a local specialist.
- You don't need to worry about overhead costs and taxes associated with employing traditional staff members.

Cons of sub-contracting:

- Finding reliable contractors isn't always easy, as scams or unreliable parties are often involved.
- It can be confusing or intimidating when working with someone with different standards or expectations than you do.
- Additional costs may be associated with sub-contracting, such as platform fees or payroll tax for a full-time employee in a foreign country.
- It may also be difficult to ensure quality control when outsourcing work, as it depends heavily on the contractor's skill level and capabilities.

Tips for Successfully Navigating Tricky Conversations With Clients

As a freelancer, you may encounter challenging or tricky situations with clients. These can range from budgets or unmet expectations to disagreement over specific project details. As a freelancer, navigating such situations and maintaining a good relationship with your client can be hard. While these conversations may be difficult, there are some key tips for handling them professionally and successfully.

1. Establish Ground Rules

Setting clear expectations between both parties is important before embarking on any project. This includes discussing deadlines and budgets and any other factors that might be at play during the project's duration. Having this information upfront will help avoid any potential issues down the line.

2. Be Proactive

Don't wait until something goes wrong to address potential problems with your client. If you spot anything that could become an issue later on, such as a budget discrepancy or timeline concerns, bring it up with the client immediately so you can come up with a solution together before it becomes an issue.

3. Communicate Openly

Communication is key when working through tricky client situations. Ensure all communication is open and honest so everyone understands where each party stands on an issue and how they could move forward together if needed. This means listening intently as well. Try to really hear what your client has to say before responding in kind, so everyone feels like they are heard before rushing into anything else prematurely.

4. Offer Solutions Instead of Problems

Don't enter into tricky conversations simply offering criticism or pointing out what won't work. Instead, focus on providing solutions that can help get both parties on the same page quickly and easily without resorting to conflict resolution tactics, often leading to more friction than progress. Doing this will show your client that you are invested in finding solutions rather than just finding ways of getting out of projects or prolonging them unnecessarily due to disagreements or issues within the constraints of the original agreement between all parties involved.

How To Adjust Your Rate As You Gain Experience

As freelancers, we often need to adjust our rates upward from time to time. As we gain experience, adjusting our rate appropriately becomes necessary to stay competitive in the market and increase our potential earnings. Here are some tips for adjusting your rate as you gain experience:

1. Research Your Market

Before modifying your rates, research the freelance rates for similar services in the area. This will give you a better idea of what your competitors are charging and what you should aim for when setting your rates.

2. Know Your Worth

When setting rates, know your worth, and don't feel like you have to charge too little if you don't feel comfortable doing so. Believe in yourself, and don't be afraid to ask for more money – after all, if you don't negotiate, no one else will!

3. Take into Account Previous Experience

If you've been freelancing for some time now and have gained valuable skills along the way, consider this when deciding on a new rate. You can also raise your price gradually over time. Doing so allows clients to get used to the new price before committing themselves long-term.

4. Be Open About It

When adjusting your rate, always let clients know about the changes that are taking place in advance, so there aren't any surprises down the line. This will also allow clients to voice any concerns regarding the new prices so that everyone is on the same page from day one.

5. Monitor Your Progress

Freelancers should keep track of the number and types of clients they have gained or lost over time due to rate changes. This will indicate how successful their rate change has been and whether it is attracting new customers or driving away existing ones. They can also track their overall financial performance over time to see if there has been any meaningful improvement since changing rates.

6. Implement Client-Specific Pricing

Client-specific pricing is a great way for freelancers to ensure that they are getting fair and equitable compensation for the work they produce. Established clients who have a successful relationship with their freelancer can stay at the original rate, while new clients can be brought on board at slightly higher rates. This allows writers to maintain their existing relationships by rewarding loyalty and earn more from newer clients by increasing the rate according to market standards.

What Happens if a Client Isn't Willing To Pay More?

As a freelancer, you often face the dilemma of keeping a client who won't pay your desired rate or cutting them loose and looking for other opportunities. While it can be tempting just to back down and keep the current client, that isn't always the best decision for you or your business in the long run. Here are some best practices when deciding whether to keep or cut a client:

- Have an Open Discussion: Before making any decisions, have an honest and open discussion with your client about why you're asking for more and what changes need to be made for them to stay within their budget. This will give both parties a chance to air out any concerns or issues that may arise and come up with alternative solutions that work for everyone involved.

- Know When To Walk Away: If, after an open discussion, your client still isn't willing to accommodate your request, it might be time to start looking elsewhere. It can be hard to walk away from a client, but if they aren't willing to pay you what you feel is fair, it might be best to look for opportunities elsewhere.

- Prioritize Your Sanity: Don't put yourself through extra stress just because someone refuses to pay you what you deem necessary. Take care of yourself first before compromising on rates of pay. Sometimes walking away from a difficult situation is worth more than staying put, especially at the expense of your mental health or other commitments.

- Know Your Value: Never settle for less than what you deserve; if a project requires significantly more effort than others, then make sure that it is reflected in the rate. Being able to recognize and value your work is essential not only as a freelancer but also as an entrepreneur as well.

The Story of Sam and Sally: How Freelance Writers Can Negotiate Better Deals

Sam was a talented freelance writer, but he lacked the confidence to demand what he deserved for his work. Whenever someone offered him a job, no matter how low the pay rate, Sam would accept it without hesitation or negotiation. He believed that his writing spoke for itself and that clients would reward him with fair compensation.

Little did Sam know, but he was leaving money on the table by accepting every offer without question. After all, there is power in negotiating better deals – something Sally understood well.

Sally was a savvy freelance writer who always sought ways to grow her business and make more money. She had done her research and knew how much she should be charging for her work based on standard rates in the market. She was never afraid to ask for what she wanted and used her knowledge of negotiation strategies to secure better wages from clients. With time and effort, she managed to increase her income from just a few thousand dollars to six figures and beyond –– achieving financial security which still serves her today.

Sam's story serves as an important reminder that even talented freelancers like himself need to practice good negotiation tactics when working with clients –– otherwise, they risk not getting the rates they deserve for their hard work.

Chapter 9 Tips for Keeping Your Clients Begging for More

As a freelance writer, I quickly learned that cultivating solid relationships with clients is essential for success. When I first entered the industry, I had to spend a lot of time hustling for new gigs. But I found that once I started producing quality work that exceeded their expectations, my clients began to spread the word about my services.

In fact, many of my clients were so impressed with my work that they left glowing 5-star reviews and testimonials across my website and social media platforms. These positive reviews played a critical role in attracting new clients and establishing myself as a trusted authority in my niche.

To maintain these relationships, I frequently communicated with my clients, keeping them updated on my progress, responding to their inquiries promptly, and addressing their concerns. I also made sure to ask for feedback on my work so that I could continually improve and exceed their expectations.

If you want to keep your clients begging for more, it's crucial to prioritize their satisfaction by taking the time to understand their needs, goals, and target audience. Deliver the work that's not only informative but also engaging and enjoyable to read. Focus on maintaining open communication channels and encouraging positive reviews and testimonials from your satisfied clients. Ultimately, your clients are your most valuable asset, and investing time in their success will ultimately pay off in the long run.

Your #1 Goal

Getting repeat business from existing clients should be the goal of every freelance writer. Working with the same clients allows you to build an ongoing relationship and learn more about them and their particular needs over time. This knowledge can make it easier for you to provide higher quality content consistently and promptly but with less effort and hours on your part. In turn, your client's satisfaction will be boosted, leading to repeat business and an increase to your bottom line.

Building strong relationships with current clients can save you from constantly looking for a new client after each project ends. This way, you'll be able to focus on delivering great work and growing your success while earning more money over time, since you won't lose productive hours prospecting. Having said that, a common dilemma experienced freelancers face is whether to accept a new client or stay within a tight circle of repeat customers.

Having the same group of reliable clients can provide a steady flow of income while also cutting down on time spent prospecting for new customers. It allows you to develop trust and build relationships with these clients who, in turn, will recommend your services to other potential customers. On the other hand, continually taking on new projects often allows for more creative opportunities and keeps the work interesting. However, it also comes with its own risks, such as not knowing how reliable the customer's payment processes may be or if they will truly value your work.

This chapter will discuss the best practices for keeping your current clients and how to make them return begging for more. We'll discuss topics such as establishing connections, focusing on the quality of work, staying up-to-date, building relationships and being accountable for any mistakes or missed deadlines. Here's a quick overview:

1. Establishing Connections

Freelancers need to stay connected with their current clients, even when no immediate work needs to be done. Proactively reaching out is also a great way to show your value and let them know they can call on you in the future. You can offer helpful advice, send links to valuable web resources, or offer free short-term projects such as white papers or report writing to demonstrate your abilities.

Being proactive in this way helps you build a good relationship and gives the client an idea of what kind of work you can provide - showing how valuable you are as a writer. Additionally, networking events, industry conferences, and workshops can all be used as opportunities to strengthen relationships and promote yourself as an expert in your field.

2. Focusing on Quality

Quality should be the main focus of all freelancer work, regardless of project size. Take time to think through each project and consider what sort of content would best answer the client's needs. For example, if they need a blog post, make sure to research related topics, come up with an engaging title and structure your piece in a way that appeals to their target market.

Be mindful of potential spelling and grammatical errors, as any mistakes can reflect poorly on your overall credibility and professionalism as a writer. Using a writing tool like Grammarly or Hemingway can be invaluable, and both are very cost-effective. Additionally, fact-check all information included in your work before you deliver it. As a freelancer, it's important to recognize that investing extra effort in ensuring each piece meets your standards will go a long way towards gaining repeat business from clients.

3. Staying Up-to-Date

Staying current on industry trends and aspects related to the work you're hired for can be a great way to differentiate yourself from other freelancers. Make sure to dedicate time each week to attend webinars, read up on relevant articles, or join discussion groups with freelancers in your field. Doing this will also help you stay informed of any changes within the industry that could affect your work.

Additionally, being actively involved in conversations regarding your area of expertise will make it easier for potential clients to find you and understand your services. Developing relationships with other freelancers is also a great option, as it allows for collaboration and insight into how others approach their projects. Being aware of all these key elements means you'll have an edge when it comes to wooing clients and staying one step ahead of the competition.

4. Building Relationships

Maintaining a positive relationship with clients is essential for setting yourself up for success in freelancing. It's important to make sure that each client feels appreciated and valued, so they come back for more work in the future. Showing appreciation can be as simple as quickly responding to questions or updating them on progress and milestones.

Don't underestimate the power of informal communication, such as sending a thank-you note or checking in with them occasionally. Doing this will set you apart from other freelancers and create trust between you and your clients. Additionally, it's also beneficial to stay in touch after projects are completed, as this can help establish strong relationships with existing clients, leading to better long-term success and career growth opportunities.

5. Being Accountable

Being accountable for mistakes and missed deadlines is key to successful freelancing. When dealing with client work, be sure to recognize any issues that may occur and address them quickly and properly. A great way to do this is by offering solutions as soon as possible, even if that means admitting mistakes or working harder than you initially anticipated.

Resolving conflicts on time ensures the client knows they can trust your service and will likely return to collaborate with you again. Additionally, take advantage of any feedback given by clients, as it helps you stay on track and improve your services in the future. Accountability doesn't just keep current clients happy; it also indicates great professionalism, which can help attract more potential customers in the long run.

Too Many, Too Few, or Just Right? Tips for Finding the Best Number of Clients for You

It's essential to create a diverse base of reliable clients who can provide steady work and compensation so that any loss of one particular client doesn't cause irreversible damage. However, having too many clients can lead to poor quality and eventual burnout, while relying on too few clients for a freelance career may also lead to problems down the line. While there's no magic number, here are some things to think about to help decide what the best number of clients is for your practice.

Dealing with Too Many Clients: How to Avoid Burnout and Maintain Your Quality Standards

As a freelance writer, the idea of having too many clients may seem like a dream come true. After all, more clients usually mean higher gross earnings. However, juggling too many clients can have a detrimental effect on your work, health, and sanity.

The Risks of Having Too Many Clients

While it may seem counterintuitive, having too many clients can actually harm your business. Here are some of the risks you should be aware of:

Overworking

Juggling multiple projects at the same time can be incredibly stressful and time-consuming. You may find yourself working long hours, weekends, and even holidays just to meet all of your clients' demands. This can lead to fatigue, burnout, and a decline in the quality of your work.

Missed Deadlines

When you have too many clients, it's easy to get overwhelmed and miss deadlines. When you miss deadlines, your clients may lose confidence in your abilities, and they may not want to work with you again in the future. This can harm your reputation and make it even more challenging to attract new clients.

Decrease in Quality

When you have too many clients, it's tough to maintain the same level of quality across all of your projects. You may rush through some of the work, skip important steps or make careless errors, resulting in a decrease in quality. This can undermine your reputation and damage your relationships with your clients.

How to Manage Too Many Clients

If you're swamped with too many clients, don't panic. Here are some strategies for managing your workload and maintaining your quality standards:

Prioritize Your Workload

Begin by separating urgent and critical projects from the routine ones. Then, create a timetable for when you will work on each project to meet its deadline. Prioritizing your workload will help you stay organized and ensure that you're completing projects on time and with the highest quality possible.

Delegate Tasks

Consider delegating some of your work to third-party contractors or assistants who can assist you with administrative tasks such as research or editing work.

Establish Boundaries

Set clear guidelines for when you will answer calls and emails, and stick to them. You can mention these guidelines in your email signature or on your website. Inform your clients of your office hours and avoid taking work home with you.

Increase Your Rates

If you're swamped with work and willing to take on less work, consider increasing your rates to reduce the amount of work assigned.

Learn to Say No

Avoid taking on more work than you can handle. It's tempting to say yes to every project that comes your way, but sometimes you need to learn to say no. There's nothing wrong with declining work that doesn't fit your expertise, schedule or rates.

Managing too many clients can be challenging, but with the right strategies, it is possible to avoid burnout and maintain your quality standards. Remember to prioritize your workload, delegate tasks, establish boundaries, increase your rates or learn to say no when necessary. By doing so, you'll be able to deliver quality work and maintain your reputation as a freelance writer.

When You Have Too Few Clients: How to Attract More Business and Diversify Your Income

As a freelance writer, having a few reliable clients to work with consistently can seem like a safe and comfortable position to be. However, relying on too few clients can make you vulnerable to market fluctuations, unexpected cancellations, and lost income.

The Risks of Having Too Few Clients

Having too few clients can be risky in several ways. Here are some of the notable risks:

Instability

If one of your few clients cancels their engagement or reduces their work, it can have a significant impact on your income and destabilize your business. Similarly, if you rely on one or two particular niches or sectors, changes in the industry or economy can negatively affect your abilities to find new business.

Limited Earnings

While working with a few clients can offer stability, it can also limit your earning potential. Without additional streams of income, you may not be earning as much as you could or as much as you'd like to, and may struggle to make ends meet.

Limited Professional Growth

Relying on too few clients can also limit your professional growth. Without exposure to a wide range of clients and projects, you run the risk of becoming stale or pigeonholed with no room for growth or development.

Tips for Attracting More Business and Diversifying Your Income

If you're struggling with a limited number of clients, here are some strategies for attracting more business and diversifying your income:

Making the Most of Social Media

Use social media to your advantage, whether through building your brand, networking, or sharing high-quality content aimed at your target clients' specific needs. Use LinkedIn, Facebook, Twitter, and Instagram to increase your visibility and connect with potential clients.

Reaching Out to Your Network

Leverage your existing network to find new work. A personal recommendation from someone you know can go a long way in securing new business. Reach out to former colleagues, peers or anyone who can refer you to their network.

Niche Down or Expand Your Expertise

Consider narrowing your focus or expanding your expertise to appeal to new clients or sectors. Use your experience and interests to corner niche markets, or seek out new industries and types of work to expand your capabilities.

Offer New Services

Consider expanding your range of services to appeal to a broader range of clients. For example, if you're a writer, you could offer editing or public relations services, in addition to other content-related projects.

Build a Sales Funnel

Build a sales funnel for your website or online presence to attract prospective clients to your services. Consider offering a free guide, e-book, or subscription to attract sign-ups and potential clients.

In summary, whether you're just starting out as a freelance writer or looking to build more sources of income, be sure to diversify your client base appropriately. Remember that having too few clients can be risky, and can limit your earnings potential and growth. Instead, use the strategies outlined above to attract a more extensive network of clients, get out of your comfort zone and take advantage of new opportunities.

Achieving the Right Balance: How to Find the

Right Number of Clients for Your Freelance Writing Business

Your ideal client load is the number of clients that you can comfortably handle without sacrificing your quality of work, endangering your health or wellbeing, or damaging your relationships with clients.

Here are a few questions to guide you in determining your optimal client load:

- What is the minimum amount of work you need to take on to meet your financial goals?
- What is the maximum amount of time you're willing to work each week?
- What are your strengths and weaknesses, and how can you use them to balance your workload?
- Are you comfortable juggling overlapping deadlines and managing multiple projects?

By taking consideration of these factors, you can begin to establish your optimal client load and aim for a balance that works best for you.

Tips for Finding the Right Balance

Here are some actionable tips to help you find the right balance:

Track Your Time

Use time-tracking software to determine how much time you're dedicating to each client and project. By tracking your time, you can discover how much time you're spending on administrative tasks, out-of-hours work or tasks that you may be inefficient at. You can then adjust your client load as needed.

Re-evaluate Your Client Base Regularly

Revisit your customer list regularly and assess if every customer aligns with your changing ambitions and financial goals. Eliminate clients that may be a bad fit for your skills or product, or freeloaders once they become more demanding than productive.

Set Boundaries

Learning how to say "no" to suitors may appear tough, but keeping your freedom, motivation, and reduced stress over the long haul is well worth it. Be explicit about work hours, availability, and turnaround times, and be willing to refer new clients to other quality practitioners.

Consider Automation

Automating the administrative tasks such as invoicing, contract management, and billing can help streamline your workflow, giving you more time to focus on producing quality work. In additional to automation, consider the possibility of delegating some of your work to other freelancers located in other parts of the world.

Diversify Your Income Streams

Diversifying your income streams can help you manage the risks of working with a select number of clients. Consider offering additional services or branching out into new markets and industries to expand your client base and overall revenue.

Conclusion

Building strong relationships with your clients is essential for success as a freelance writer. Remember to prioritize their satisfaction, communicate openly, and seek feedback to improve your work continually. Getting repeat business from existing clients can lead to positive reviews, testimonials, and referrals, which can attract new clients and establish your authority as a trusted writer in your niche.

At the same time, finding the right balance of clients is also crucial. Overbooking yourself can lead to burnout and lower quality work, while having too few clients can limit your earning potential and growth. By prioritizing your workload, setting boundaries, and diversifying your income streams, you can achieve the optimal client load for your freelance writing business.

Ultimately, keeping your clients begging for more requires consistent effort, attention to detail, and an unwavering commitment to quality. By following the tips outlined in this chapter, you'll set yourself up for long-term success as a freelance writer and cultivate a loyal base of clients who appreciate your hard work and dedication.

Chapter 10 Simple Mindset Shifts To Help You Handle Rejection and Criticism

Rejection is a natural part of the freelance writing industry, and many writers experience multiple rejections before they receive their first paid job. This string of rejections can be disheartening and take a toll on a writer's self-confidence. However, some everyday people have shown how to overcome these challenges and achieve success.

Mark Manson is a NY Times best-selling author, self-help blogger, and personal development consultant. His journey as a writer is full of rejections before tasting success. He flunked out of law school, could not sustain employment, and was rejected by publishers for years before becoming a well-known author.

Lin Manuel Mirando is an American composer, lyricist, playwright, rapper, and actor. He is best known for creating and starring in the hit Broadway musicals "In The Heights" and "Hamilton". Despite his success now, he had to face several rejections and failures in the initial stages of his career.

Mirando faced several years of rejections and failures before gaining any recognition. His musicals got rejected by many theatres and investors, and many believed he was likely going to fail. Instead of giving up, he believed in himself and his unique ideas and kept pushing himself forward.

These are just two examples. It's important to remember that rejection isn't necessarily indicative of your talent or capability as a professional writer - it simply means that your work didn't fit the job description in this particular instance. By understanding that failure is an inevitable part of every creative journey, you can use these moments of rejection to fuel your passion and propel yourself forward, allowing them to become learning experiences rather than sources of discouragement.

Fortunately, with the right mindset shifts, you can learn to navigate these challenges confidently and resiliently. This chapter will explore simple ways to handle rejection and criticism to promote personal growth and success in freelancing. We'll examine how fear of rejection or criticism can impede professional progress. Next, we'll consider strategies for reframing failure as a learning opportunity and leveraging mistakes for future successes. Additionally, we'll discuss how cultivating self-empathy, embracing constructive feedback, and finding strength in vulnerability can help writers face criticism head-on.

Understanding and Overcoming Fear of Rejection or Criticism

Fear of rejection and criticism is a natural reaction for many freelance writers, but it's important to understand that these emotions don't have to be paralyzing. One way to start overcoming your fear of rejection or criticism is by reframing failure as an opportunity for growth. Instead of viewing a rejection or negative feedback as the end of the road, you can view it as an informative experience that can help you take steps towards improving and progressing in your writing journey.

When reframing failure as an opportunity for growth, it's important to remember that it's okay to make mistakes. After all, everyone faced failures and setbacks at some point in their lives. Instead of beating yourself over the rejection, focus on the knowledge that you can gain from the experience.

For example, if you receive negative feedback from a client or editor, take a step back and ask yourself, "What can I learn from this?" By shifting your perspective from the negative elements of rejection, you gain a learning opportunity and have a chance to improve your skills.

Another way to reframe failure as an opportunity for growth is to set realistic goals. Instead of focusing on outcomes that may be out of your control, such as getting published in a particular magazine, focus on what you can do to improve your writing skills. You can set attainable goals, such as writing one piece a day or reading two books on the topic weekly. Trying again, despite previous rejections, will not only take you closer to your target but also improve your writing skills along the way.

Another effective strategy for confronting any feelings of apprehension is self-empathy. Regularly practicing self-compassion and kindness will remind you that making mistakes doesn't mean you're incompetent. It simply means that you're human, and striving for perfection all the time is an impossible task that nobody could ever meet. By treating yourself with patience and empathy when faced with rejections or criticism, this understanding will allow you to focus on growing rather than dwelling on any perceived setbacks.

Finally, learning to deal with critique healthily is also essential in overcoming the fear of rejection or criticism. Embracing both positive and constructive feedback allows writers to refine their craft and learn from each experience continuously—positive or negative—moving forward in their writing career. Accepting feedback can feel challenging at first, but it's one of the best ways to remain open-minded when faced with criticism so that we can use it to better ourselves rather than stagnate in our writing development.

Developing Resilience Through Self-Reflection

As freelance writers, resilience is a crucial part of success. With the often unpredictable and fast-paced nature of the industry, it's important to withstand disappointments and remain motivated to push forward despite any obstacles that may arise. Self-reflection is an effective tool for building this much-needed trait.

One of the most powerful benefits of self-reflection for freelance writers is identifying potential growth areas. By examining your past experiences and analyzing how your actions influenced different outcomes, you can gain valuable insight into where improvement is necessary to succeed. This practice also allows you to acknowledge your strengths and recognize the efforts behind your accomplishments – fostering an understanding that failure doesn't define you as a writer, but hard work and dedication do.

Another way self-reflection aids in building resilience among freelance writers is through instilling inner confidence. Looking back at their prior successes helps writers understand that their current setback does not define them as a whole. Instead, it reminds them of their capabilities when challenged with difficult tasks. Additionally, reflecting on lessons learned from shortcomings helps build resilience by showing how even failure can be used constructively toward growth. Doing so allows writers to embrace mistakes rather than fearing them and eventually lead toward victory instead.

Finally, taking time out for regular self-reflection gives freelance writers much-needed space to reflect on their goals without feeling rushed or pressured by external influences such as deadlines or clients' expectations. Doing so gives these individuals enough time to recharge themselves and reconnect with what motivates them — making it easier for them to regain their motivation after any discouraging events they may face while working on projects. Self-reflection helps freelance writers cultivate resilience by providing an opportunity for both introspection and appreciation — reminding us that our failures aren't indicative of our worth but rather a step towards progressing further down our creative paths.

Learning From Mistakes and Embracing Failure

Mistakes are inevitable in a freelance writing business, no matter how seasoned the writer is. Common missteps writers make include taking on too many projects at once, not charging enough for their work or services, and not accounting for additional expenses such as taxes or software subscriptions. Aspiring and veteran writers alike should create a schedule for themselves to ensure they don't overextend themselves or burn out from being overly ambitious. Additionally, making sure to research industry rates and account for any business costs will help prevent financial insecurity in the future.

But more importantly, embracing failure is one of the best ways to prevent these mistakes from happening again. Freelance writers should look back at their experiences with honesty and compassion to identify causes of failure while continuing to nurture their creative skill sets. This self-reflection allows them to become aware of areas where improvement is needed — whether it's managing projects better or building stronger relationships with clients — ultimately helping them progress in their freelancing journey.

At the end of the day, falling short on a project or choosing the wrong client isn't necessarily negative. It can be an opportunity for growth if you allow yourself to learn from your missteps rather than letting it bring you down. Learning how to handle mistakes constructively can help develop resilience against future failures, allowing freelance writers to stay motivated despite any obstacles that may arise during their career path. Taking time for self-reflection is essential for us to become mindful of our decisions and actions, leading us closer to success even after stumbling blocks along the way.

Making Constructive Feedback a Tool for Growth

Constructive feedback is a powerful tool for growth, especially in the freelance writing industry. Knowing how to differentiate this type of feedback from a non-constructive one helps freelance writers take advantage of these opportunities more effectively. Constructive feedback offers an honest but supportive perspective that can help people identify their weaknesses and address them accordingly — while non-constructive criticism only brings down morale and cultivates false insecurity.

As a freelancer, it's essential to solicit constructive feedback from clients to improve your writing skills. However, it can be challenging to ask for criticism without implying that you didn't do an excellent job. One way to frame feedback constructively is by positioning it as an opportunity to improve your writing skills rather than criticism of your performance. You can use phrases such as "I welcome your feedback so I can continue to enhance my skills" or "Please let me know how I can improve for future projects."

Another strategy to consider is using neutral language that doesn't imply fault or blame. Instead of asking, "What did I do wrong?" try asking, "What could I have done differently to improve the work?" This approach shifts the focus from your performance to the outcome of the project.

When receiving feedback, listen actively without getting defensive, and ask for clarification if needed. Restate the feedback to ensure you understand it correctly, and acknowledge the client's point of view. Show gratitude to the client for taking the time to review your work, whether the feedback is positive or negative. By following these approaches, you can solicit constructive feedback without implying that you failed in your current project.

The key to making constructive feedback work as a growth tool lies in how it's processed. Freelance writers need to be open-minded when dealing with any criticism so they can take the opportunity to improve their craft or develop new skills if needed. For example, if a client provides constructive feedback on a writer's work, such as pointing out areas of improvement for clarity or style, then taking that advice into account is essential for the writer to succeed.

Additionally, embracing other people's opinions and being humble enough to accept critiques also helps build stronger relationships with clients as well. Rather than feeling insulted or disheartened by critique, use it as an invitation to develop your skillset further, demonstrating your professionalism and eagerness to learn throughout your career path. Doing so reinforces trust between yourself and others you collaborate with.

Overall, receiving positive or negative comments is simply part of being a freelance writer. But learning how to turn constructive feedback into a valuable asset makes all the difference in achieving success within our respective fields. Making constructive criticism work for us rather than feeling intimidated by it allows us to grow much faster towards attaining our professional goals while inspiring us towards personal improvement.

Fostering a Positive Attitude Toward Setbacks

Simon Sinek is a motivational speaker, popular author, and marketing consultant known for his leadership and personal growth theories. Over the years, he has delivered powerful talks on fostering positive attitudes towards setbacks.

Sinek believes that we often misunderstand the concept of leadership and failure. According to him, true leadership isn't about being perfect; instead, it is about learning and growing from our mistakes. Sinek encourages people to adopt a growth mindset when dealing with setbacks- see them as opportunities to learn and grow rather than as roadblocks to success.

In his talks, Sinek often cites personal stories of failures in his life, indicating that it's natural to experience setbacks while pursuing one's goals. He often encourages audiences to view failures in a more productive light, such as an indication of the areas that need improving, hindrances that have been removed from their path, etc. This approach allows people to evaluate their actions and adjust accordingly, setting them up for better chances of success in future endeavors.

As a freelance writer, setbacks and failures are unavoidable. It's important to understand that these challenging moments in our careers are essential for growth and should be embraced rather than feared. Fostering a positive attitude towards setbacks can help us learn from our mistakes and maximize our chances of success in the long run.

The first step towards achieving this is having the right mentality when dealing with failure. Keeping an open mind instead of feeling overwhelmed by failure will help us focus on what went wrong while maintaining productivity — allowing us to take actionable steps instead of getting stuck in a negative cycle. Additionally, taking time to reflect on why certain projects didn't work out is an invaluable improvement tool. It lets us identify what we could have done better so that we can apply different approaches or methods next time for better results.

Additionally, it's important to maintain self-compassion when dealing with failure. Separating yourself from your missteps and looking at them objectively will help you detach from any sense of shame or guilt associated with shortcomings, further inspiring you towards progress instead of dragging you down into discouragement or disappointment.

This doesn't mean that we should avoid responsibility. On the contrary, constantly using our mistakes to improve ourselves is key to success in our respective fields.

Ultimately, success as a freelance writer isn't about perfection but rather how willing you are to take risks and make mistakes to grow your skillset and gain experience along the way. That's why fostering an open, positive attitude towards setbacks is crucial for generating momentum throughout our professional journeys.

Appreciating Criticism as an Opportunity To Learn

Criticism is often viewed as a negative thing, but it can actually be an excellent opportunity to learn and grow. As a freelance writer, it's important to embrace criticism with an open mind and appreciation. Seeing critique as a valuable tool for improvement helps us take advantage of the newfound knowledge that comes out of it.

One way writers can use criticism as an opportunity to learn is by taking it as part of the creative process. Critique should be seen as part of the journey, inspiring us to continue striving towards bettering ourselves — rather than feeling discouraged or frustrated by it. Asking questions to gain further insight from our critics also helps develop our analytical skills and strengthen our understanding of different aspects of our craft, leading to more well-rounded results in future projects.

Furthermore, acknowledging mistakes and using them as a learning experience by reflecting on what went wrong or how things could have been improved allows us to use any feedback constructively instead of letting ourselves get weighed down by disappointment. This type of self-reflection can ultimately help enhance your writing skills in the long run.

Learning to appreciate criticism enables freelance writers to become even stronger professionals while inspiring personal growth by applying new insights and knowledge. Allowing yourself to be open and receptive to critiques is an invaluable source of information and a much-needed reminder that having flaws or making mistakes isn't necessarily something negative — but simply a part of developing professionally and personally.

Conclusion: Embracing Constructive Criticism

In conclusion, embracing constructive criticism is an essential part of the writing journey. Feedback from clients, editors, and peers can help you grow and develop your skills as a writer. It's natural to feel apprehensive about receiving feedback, but these feelings shouldn't stop you from seeking it out.

If you find yourself struggling to accept feedback, remember to approach criticism with a growth mindset. Reframe it as an opportunity to learn and improve, rather than a personal attack on your abilities. Additionally, make sure to be specific when asking for feedback, provide a secure space for clients to share their views, and express gratitude for their support.

Remember, criticism is not a reflection of your self-worth, and accepting it doesn't mean you have failed. It's the first step towards improvement and taking your writing career to the next level. With a little bit of practice, you can develop the ability to handle constructive criticism with grace and use it to learn and grow as a writer.

Chapter 11 Time Management Strategies for Freelance Writers

As a freelance content creator, you only have so many hours in the day to get your work done. That's why effectively managing your time is crucial to your success, especially if your goal is to earn a six-figure income. Without a plan for managing your time, it's easy to get bogged down in projects, waste time on unproductive tasks, and ultimately miss out on potential opportunities.

Successful freelance writers understand that every moment of their day counts. They prioritize their time to make the most of their workday, optimize their productivity, and find a work-life balance that allows them to achieve their goals while still having time to pursue their passions. In this chapter, we'll explore some of the most effective time management strategies that freelance writers can use to stay on track, set goals, and build a thriving freelance writing career.

1. Setting Goals

Setting goals is a key component of successful time management for freelance writers. Creating achievable yet ambitious goals for yourself throughout the week or month can help you stay organized and increase your productivity.

When establishing a goal-setting strategy, it is important to set short, medium, and long-range goals. Short-term goals should be easily attainable, such as completing a certain amount of work by the end of the day or week. Medium-range goals should be more challenging but still achievable; these could include submitting assignments or landing new clients by certain deadlines. Long-range goals could include reaching certain revenue milestones or completing a specific number of projects over the year.

Setting and achieving these types of goals will help freelance writers stay focused on their tasks at hand and increase their client satisfaction rates in the long run. When someone sets specific goals for themselves and meets them successfully, they produce higher quality content with fewer mistakes from rushing through it. In addition, setting concrete targets helps keep freelancers motivated while working towards achieving their bigger dreams. It may be hard at first, but once someone sees results from setting goals and sticking to them, their confidence in themselves will grow along with their career success.

The SMART Goal Setting Strategy

The SMART goal setting strategy is a popular method for setting and achieving goals. It provides a clear framework to help you create goals that are specific, measurable, achievable, relevant, and time-bound. Here's how each step of the SMART strategy works:

Specific

Specific goals are clear and well-defined. They are not vague or subject to interpretation, which makes it easier to track progress and make adjustments. To create a specific goal, ask yourself: What do I want to accomplish? What steps do I need to take to get there?

Measurable

Measurable goals are quantifiable. They include specific metrics that allow you to track your progress and evaluate success. To make your goals measurable, ask yourself: How will I know when I've achieved my goal? What metrics will I use to assess success?

Achievable

Achievable goals are realistic and attainable. They should challenge you, but not be so far outside of your reach that they feel unattainable. To make your goals achievable, ask yourself: Is this goal within my control? Do I have the resources, skills, and support to achieve this goal?

Relevant

Relevant goals are connected to your larger vision and values. They should align with your overall career and personal objectives. To make your goals relevant, ask yourself: Why is this goal important to me? How does it add value to my career or personal life?

Time-bound

Time-bound goals are specific and have a deadline. They help you stay focused and hold yourself accountable for achieving your objectives. To make your goals time-bound, ask yourself: When do I want to achieve this goal? Is this deadline realistic given my other obligations?

By following the SMART goal setting strategy, you can create goals that are specific, measurable, achievable, relevant, and time-bound. These goals will help you stay focused and motivated as you work towards building a thriving freelance writing career.

Other Strategies for Setting Goals

Here are a few more goal setting strategies you may find useful:

OKRs

"Objectives and Key Results" (OKRs) is a goal setting system used by many successful companies. It involves setting high-level objectives and defining measurable key results that indicate progress towards achieving those objectives. The OKR system promotes alignment across teams and departments, boosts employee engagement and motivation, and improves transparency and accountability.

BHAGs

A "Big Hairy Audacious Goal" (BHAG) is an audacious long-term goal that inspires and motivates you to work towards achieving it. BHAGs typically require significant effort and investment but can lead to breakthroughs in your career or personal life. Setting a BHAG can motivate you to challenge yourself and push beyond your limitations.

WOOP

"WOOP" stands for "Wish, Outcome, Obstacle, Plan." This goal setting strategy involves visualizing your desired outcome, reflecting on any obstacles that may hinder you, and creating specific action steps to overcome these obstacles. WOOP can help you prepare for challenges and create a comprehensive plan for achieving your goals.

By exploring different goal setting strategies, freelance writers can find a system that works best for them and helps them achieve their goals.

2. Prioritizing Tasks

Prioritizing tasks is essential for freelance writers when it comes to time management. When there are competing deadlines, long-term business objectives, and limited amounts of time in the day, it is important to prioritize what is most urgent and important to maximize efficiency and income.

The best practice for a freelance writer when prioritizing tasks is to list everything they need to complete with deadlines and notes concerning their importance. This way, they can easily identify which tasks take priority over others at a glance and arrange them accordingly.

In addition to creating a list of tasks with deadlines and notes concerning their importance, various tools and software are available for freelancers to utilize when trying to prioritize and schedule their tasks. Popular task management programs such as Trello, Asana, or Monday provide easy-to-use organizational systems that help break projects down into smaller, more manageable pieces and monitor progress across multiple assignments. Their built-in features, such as labels, reminders, dashboards, and drag-and-drop functions, make it much easier for freelance writers to stay organized.

Calendar applications like Google Calendar or Outlook can be connected with these task management tools to easily create deadlines that will remind the freelancer when each item is due. They will also allow them to customize notifications, so they know exactly when they need to complete something while allowing some flexibility around other priorities.

Freelancers should also consider project flow tracking tools such as Float or Timely, which help manage their workloads over time by providing comprehensive insights into each process step — from planning to execution — to ensure that all tasks are efficiently tracked. These tools allow adjustments to be made along the way if needed while keeping an overall view of where each assignment stands in terms of completion. Once the list is created, the freelancer should focus on one task at a time rather than attempting to juggle multiple tasks simultaneously. Staying organized will help prevent missed deadlines or lost opportunities, which can negatively affect the quality of work and client satisfaction rates.

If the freelance writer finds that they have taken on too much work without enough time in the day, there are several steps they can take to address this issue:

- The first would be delegating work if possible; outsourcing certain assignments or hiring someone temporary can lighten the workload without sacrificing quality or accuracy.
- If this isn't an option, taking breaks throughout the day as needed can help keep energy levels up while allowing them to finish their duties efficiently.
- Finally, if all else fails and a deadline simply cannot be met by themselves alone, they may consider discussing it directly with their client — providing an explanation as well as possible alternatives — so that future projects are not affected by the inability to fulfill one assignment on time.

Strategies for Prioritizing Tasks

There are also several popular strategies for prioritizing tasks:

Eisenhower Matrix

The Eisenhower Matrix is a four-quadrant tool that helps you prioritize tasks based on their urgency and importance:

- Quadrant 1 includes urgent and important tasks that need to be done immediately.
- Quadrant 2 includes important but not urgent tasks that require planning and long-term thinking.
- Quadrant 3 includes urgent but not important tasks that can

be delegated.
- Finally, quadrant 4 includes tasks that are neither urgent nor important and can be eliminated or postponed.

ABC Method

The ABC method involves categorizing tasks based on their priority. Tasks are categorized as A, B, or C based on their importance. A tasks are the most important and need to be completed first. B tasks are important but not as pressing and can be done after the A tasks. C tasks are the least important and can be done after completing the A and B tasks.

Eat the Frog

The "Eat the Frog" method involves tackling the most difficult or unpleasant task first. By completing the most challenging task at the beginning of the day, you can alleviate stress and free up more time for other tasks.

Pareto Analysis

The Pareto Analysis, also known as the 80/20 rule, involves focusing on the 20% of tasks that will generate 80% of your results. By identifying the most significant tasks that can have the greatest impact, you can prioritize your time for maximum productivity and efficiency.

3. Managing Deadlines

Establishing efficient and effective deadlines is a critical skill for freelance writers, as it can make or break their ability to generate income. Without a solid plan in place to manage these deadlines, freelancers risk missing client expectations and not meeting their own financial goals.

When setting deadlines for themselves, professional writers should always be realistic about how long it will take to complete each assignment. This means taking into account how complex the task is, how long it typically takes them to finish similar projects in the past, and what other priorities are on their plate at the same time. If multiple competing assignments are due around the same time, they may need to make difficult choices regarding which ones should take priority over others. Being comfortable with making these tough calls is essential to succeed in this business.

Freelance writers can also set standards for themselves regarding when they would like to finish an assignment. For example, completing smaller tasks within 24-48 hours while reserving longer projects for weekend work that can be completed over several days or even weeks if necessary. Breaking down large projects into smaller pieces can help make them more manageable while still staying on pace with the required output levels.

In addition, setting reasonable and attainable goals throughout each assignment is a great way for freelancers to measure their progress without feeling overwhelmed or distracted by non-work-related activities. For example, if writing a blog post requires research, then setting mini milestones every day or two will help keep them motivated and on track toward completing the entire article well before its actual due date.

Finally, professional writers should strive to give themselves some extra buffer room when calculating how long it will take them to complete a project. This means having realistic expectations about the maximum amount of time it might take rather than pushing too hard, which could result in either poor quality work or missed deadlines (or both!).

Additionally, they should communicate directly with clients before accepting any assignment so that appropriate timelines are agreed upon upfront and no surprises occur along the way, which could ultimately lead to frustration or dissatisfaction down the road.

4. Scheduling Breaks

Scheduling breaks is an essential part of any freelance writer's workflow. Not only does it allow them to step away from their desk and relax, but it can also help prevent burnout and keep energy levels up for difficult assignments. Whether it be physical activity, socializing with friends, or simply reading a book — taking regular breaks can aid in producing quality work while keeping stress levels low.

For those who find it hard to switch off from work mode and take some time away, setting alarms or reminders throughout the day is a great way to ensure that breaks are actually taken. This doesn't necessarily have to be a long break from work, but even smaller periods like 5-10 minutes can help recharge the mind and bring clarity when tackling more complex tasks.

Additionally, incorporating specific activities into each break allows greater concentration and focus on projects that require more thought or mental effort. For instance, going for a walk outside or engaging in light physical exercise can help keep both productivity and creativity high since getting active has been proven to increase dopamine levels — resulting in improved memory recall and creative problem-solving abilities. If you're not familiar with it, dopamine is a neurotransmitter responsible for producing feelings of pleasure and motivation.

The same goes for using scheduled breaks to socialize with friends or family. This could involve having lunch with someone at least once per week or making plans with local contacts specializing in similar fields of expertise. Events like these provide a much-needed respite from freelancing and help build meaningful relationships, which may be useful down the road.

In addition to ensuring regular breaks are taken throughout the day, freelance writers should also consider setting aside larger chunks of time specifically devoted to rest, during which all devices are put away so that complete relaxation can occur. Whether this means completely unplugging from work-related matters for full days out of each week or even taking a few weeks off intermittently throughout the year — such periods of downtime will provide an invaluable source of energy which can then be used towards future assignments once they return to their desks refreshed and recharged.

5. Focus Blocks

As a freelance writer, you can benefit from using focus blocks in your workflow. A focus block is a fixed period of time that you dedicate to a particular task or assignment. This can be anything from research, writing, editing, or proofreading- any process involved in creating and completing a project.

By creating focus blocks, you minimize distractions such as notifications, emails, and phone calls, allowing you to dive into your work without switching between various tasks every few minutes. Additionally, scheduling smaller blocks throughout the day makes it easier to manage your workload while taking regular breaks to maintain productivity and improve concentration levels.

For example, you could set aside specific hours every morning or afternoon dedicated solely to completing research-related assignments without any external interference. You could turn off WiFi or temporarily disable notifications, allowing you to stay focused entirely on the matter at hand.

Similarly, designated writing sessions during which all other projects are put aside could help break down large tasks into manageable chunks while still allowing you to meet deadlines and make sure commitments are met.

In addition, creating uninterrupted blocks of time devoted to proofreading and editing can help you produce higher-quality work-resulting in greater client satisfaction. It is essential to have enough self-control to avoid jumping between various open documents to stay on track with the assignment being tackled at the present moment, which can be challenging when days feel like they're overflowing with personal and professional responsibilities.

Finally, scheduling some quiet and enjoyable breaks within each session is also an important part of maximizing concentration levels and energy spent on tasks throughout the day. Whether it be getting up from your desk for a short walk outside or taking a quick nap if needed, these moments serve as a way to recharge and as a potential source of inspiration if used wisely.

6. Working In Batches

Working in batches can be an incredibly effective way to maximize your efficiency and get more done in minimal time. By grouping tasks that require similar resources or have related objectives, you can stay focused on the task at hand instead of switching gears multiple times throughout your workday.

For example, you could use batching to complete a series of blog posts within one sitting. Start by gathering all research materials and developing outlines for each piece before actually writing out the content itself. This allows you to create a "flow," saving time during each stage of the process without sacrificing quality. The more efficient you are in executing tasks, the easier it is to remain consistent over time.

Another example could involve business-related assignments such as client communications or invoicing. Batching these tasks can help streamline your operations overall, freeing up time for more intense projects later on. Rather than dealing with these emails separately every few days, you can answer multiple inquiries or reminders in one go, reducing context switching and improving accuracy.

Overall, working in batches offers an array of benefits, such as uninterrupted periods of focus that can lead to greater creativity and improved accuracy. By taking advantage of this technique, you can give your best effort towards any given task without worrying about being interrupted along the way.

7. Using Resources Efficiently

Using resources efficiently is an important part of any freelancer's workflow, and having the right tools in place can make a world of difference. Timers, planners, notification systems, and automation applications are great ways to keep things organized and reduce wasted effort — so let's look at what each has to offer.

Timers

Timers are excellent for helping you stay productive by providing reminders throughout the day when it's time to switch tasks or take a break. In addition, timers can measure how long specific tasks take to estimate time for future projects better. Popular timer apps include RescueTime, Focus Booster, and Clockify — all of which provide helpful features such as tracking time spent on activities, setting goals and reminders, and reporting progress over time.

Planners

Planners can help you be more organized by providing an overview of due dates, events and other important details. For instance, Calendly allows you to sync their calendars with clients while also managing availability. By doing so, you can easily see what's coming up and prioritize accordingly without constantly referring back through emails for confirmation. Similarly, Google Calendar allows users to schedule personal projects alongside client duties to keep everything streamlined yet still visible at the same time.

Notification Systems

Notification systems can be extremely helpful in keeping focused by actively sending out updates regarding deadlines or upcoming responsibilities directly into inboxes – essentially eliminating the need to continuously check multiple sources regularly. Some popular programs that do this include Slack Notifications, which sends notifications based on user-defined triggers and IFTTT (If This Then That), which uses "recipes" created by users that receive information from multiple sources and then deliver alerts according to specified criteria.

Automation Applications

Finally, we have automation applications that are invaluable in ensuring that repetitive tasks don't become too tedious or time-consuming. Programs like Zapier allow users to set up automated workflows between different systems, such as email marketing platforms or customer relationship management systems — meaning no more manually entering data every few days. In addition, there's also Hootsuite, which simplifies social media posting by scheduling posts from sites such as Twitter and LinkedIn. Buffer also lets users create custom post schedules that submit content automatically on their behalf at designated times during the day.

All of these tools can go a long way in streamlining processes for freelance writers to remain productive while maintaining a healthy balance between work and other commitments outside of their work life.

Conclusion: Key Takeaways

As a freelance writer, effectively managing your time is crucial to your success and earning a six-figure income. By implementing various time management strategies, you can maximize your efficiency, stay focused, and achieve your career and personal objectives. Here are some key takeaways:

- The SMART goal setting strategy is a helpful framework for setting specific, measurable, achievable, relevant, and time-bound goals.
- Prioritizing tasks using strategies such as the Eisenhower Matrix, ABC method, Eat the Frog, and Pareto Analysis can help you manage your workload effectively.
- Working in batches can streamline operations, allowing you to complete tasks more efficiently and improve accuracy.
- Focus blocks are fixed periods of time you dedicate to a particular task or assignment, minimizing distractions and allowing you to stay focused.
- Taking breaks within each session is also an essential part of maximizing concentration levels and energy spent on tasks throughout the day.

By implementing these strategies, you can succeed as a freelance writer and achieve your financial goals. Remember, effective time management is crucial to building a successful and fulfilling career in freelance writing.

Chapter 12 Growing Your Freelance Writing Business

Earning six figures as a freelancer is an admirable achievement - and there is absolutely nothing wrong with continuing to work independently if that's what you prefer. Many writers have found success through this route, building their businesses and enjoying the freedom of working on their own terms.

However, as a freelance writer, the biggest challenge in growing your business is the fact that you must do everything yourself. It can be difficult to scale your business if you are always the only one doing the work. This can lead to overworking yourself, burnout, and ultimately, a stagnation in your business growth.

But, there are freelancers who have found ways to grow their business while still providing top-notch service to their clients. For instance, take my friend Sarah, who was struggling to find enough time to accomplish everything she needed to do to get her business to the next level. Being a perfectionist, she wanted to make sure her clients were always getting the best of her talents— every second of the day.

Sarah soon realized that, as much as she wanted to do everything herself, it would be impossible to grow her business if she had to handle everything alone. She started delegating some of the work, hired some freelancers, and outsourced some of the operations she felt were not her strengths. This move not only freed up more of her own time, but it also allowed her more time to develop the direction of her business, while she trusted others to take care of the smaller details.

This strategy allowed her to grow her business and take on more clients, all while maintaining the level of quality her clients expected from her. She also found that by working with other freelancers, it was easier to collaborate on projects and leverage the strengths of her team members.

So, while the challenge of growing your freelance writing business may seem insurmountable, it is possible to achieve success. By delegating tasks, collaborating with others, and focusing on what truly adds value to your business, you too can achieve growth while maintaining the level of quality your clients expect.

This chapter will explore different strategies for growing a freelance writing business and taking it to the next level. For those already earning six figures through freelance writing, there are ways to double or even triple your income. We will explore topics such as outsourcing opportunities, utilizing paid advertising platforms, developing structured content strategies, and exploring different freelance writing business models.

By the end of this chapter, you'll have an in-depth understanding of all the methods you can use to maximize your success as a freelancer without sacrificing your independence or creativity.

Exploring Outsourcing Opportunities

By taking advantage of virtual assistants, freelancers can free up their time and increase their efficiency, while leveraging freelance marketplaces allows them to find the right talent for their projects quickly. In this section, we will take an in-depth look at both of these subtopics so that you can make sure your business is running at its best.

We will explore how to find and hire quality virtual assistants and use them effectively, as well as how to navigate the various freelance marketplaces online. We'll also provide tips on identifying great potential assistant freelancers and ensuring they have the skills and qualifications required for the job. With this knowledge, you can confidently move forward with your outsourcing initiatives and take your freelance writing business to new heights.

Utilizing Virtual Assistants to Free Up Your Time and Increase Your Efficiency

By taking advantage of virtual assistant services, a freelancer can manage multiple clients, create content plans, keep up with industry trends, improve marketing techniques, and more. To ensure the greatest success when using VAs, here are some best practices to consider:

- Identify the skillset needed in a VA to find one or more who fit your job requirements perfectly.
- Have clear expectations and processes regarding communication and delegation, so everyone knows what's expected of them.
- Take advantage of trial periods or other testing means before hiring a VA.
- Make sure you have a contingency plan should your VA not be able to fulfill their duties for any reason.
- Establish an onboarding process to ensure new VAs understand your business objectives and how they will help achieve them.

By following these best practices, you can confidently move forward with your outsourcing initiatives knowing that you've done your due diligence in finding the right people for the job. The advantages of using virtual assistants include being able to scale quickly and easily while focusing on building up quality relationships with clients, improving overall productivity by delegating mundane tasks away from yourself, and taking pressure off of yourself as an individual freelancer by having an additional resource (or resources) available at all times.

One of the potential drawbacks to using virtual assistants is that you may spend more time managing them than producing quality content for their clients. This can happen when expectations and processes are not clearly established or communicated beforehand. To avoid this, it's important that a freelancer takes the time to carefully evaluate and understand the skillset they need in a VA - this could mean hiring someone with a specialized set of skills if that's necessary. It is also helpful to have an onboarding process so new VAs understand your business objectives and how they will help achieve them. Additionally, establish a clear communication plan while delegating tasks so everyone involved understands what's expected of them.

Another potential drawback is trusting another person with sensitive information and giving them access to important accounts, such as social media profiles or private documents. Before hiring, make sure you vet the VA thoroughly - do an online search to see if there are any issues associated with the VA, ask for references from previous employers, and don't be afraid to negotiate your own agreement regarding confidentiality and liability. Doing these things can help mitigate risk and ensure you get reliable services from trustworthy people.

Finally, make sure you have a contingency plan should your VA not be able to fulfill their duties for any reason. Develop backup plans by outlining tasks you can quickly complete in case of emergency or sudden incapacity of your VA. Doing so will prepare you to handle anything that comes up without impacting client deadlines or other important deliverables.

Leveraging Freelance Marketplaces and Finding the Right Talent for Your Projects

Once you've determined the type of virtual assistant needed, the next step is identifying the right talent for their projects. Numerous freelance marketplaces online make it easy to connect with VAs and post job listings. Some popular sites include Upwork, Fiverr, Guru, and Freelancer.com. It's important to look at a VA's portfolio and read their reviews before making a hiring decision, as this will provide you with more insight into their skillset and how reliable they might be.

It can also be helpful to take advantage of trial periods or other means of testing before committing to hiring someone. This allows for a better evaluation of the VA's specific skillset and demonstrates how well they communicate and work within your business structure. Additionally, many agencies offer packages designed specifically for hiring virtual assistants. These can be beneficial if you need help finding multiple people with specialized skill sets in different areas, such as social media marketing or content creation.

When looking for a VA on freelance marketplaces, try setting up calls or interviews with potential candidates so you can get more information about their experience and find out what kind of questions they feel qualified to answer. Keep in mind that quality VAs may command higher rates than those who are less experienced or have fewer skills. Of course, when hiring talented VAs at these higher rates, you should expect outstanding results from them.

In addition to leveraging freelance marketplaces, there are other effective ways of finding skilled VAs. For example, through referrals from other professionals or by joining industry networks like Facebook groups or job-specific Slack channels where members share resources like contacts or advice about working with virtual assistants. Taking time to research thoroughly is crucial. No matter which route a freelancer chooses for finding the right VA for their project, understanding what each site offers can go a long way in ensuring that you pick the most competent candidate available.

For freelancers based in the United States, virtual assistants located in other countries can have pros and cons. On the one hand, hiring international VAs may mean lower rates due to a lower cost of living, fluctuations in currency exchange rates, and increased competition for talent. Additionally, working with someone from a different culture can be incredibly rewarding and educational. It can provide new perspectives on work practices and challenge how you view your professional processes.

On the downside, there are a few challenges to consider when working with international VAs, such as language barriers, time zone differences, and unreliable internet or power service. This can lead to communication issues or missed deadlines if expectations and processes are not properly established beforehand. To help avoid this, make sure you thoroughly research potential overseas candidates to get a better understanding of their skillset and experience level. It's also important to develop a clear communication plan, including setting expectations regarding response times and availability while considering different time zones and cultural customs.

Utilizing Paid Advertising Platforms To Reach New Audiences

Paid advertising is essential to any digital marketing strategy, as it allows freelancers and businesses to target new audiences and drive traffic to their websites. You can effectively reach new customers and increase online visibility by utilizing paid advertising platforms such as Google Ads and Facebook Ads.

When developing a paid advertising plan, there are many things to consider, such as exploring different options, crafting unique ad copy that stands out from the competition, and creating specialized funnels for maximum conversion rate.

Exploring Different Paid Advertising Options

There are many paid advertising options to consider, such as Google Ads, Facebook Ads, Bing Ads, LinkedIn Ads, Twitter Ads, Instagram Ads, YouTube Ads and many more. Depending on your goals as a freelancer and the desired audience you hope to reach, it is important to evaluate your options carefully before deciding. Each platform has its features that may not be necessary or beneficial for every situation.

When selecting the right paid advertising option, there are a few best practices that should be followed:

- Research who you're targeting and tailor your message accordingly – this could include creating multiple versions of ads targeting different demographics or interests.
- Craft creative copy that stands out from your competition – this could mean investing in unique visuals or writing unique ad copy that speaks directly to potential customers.
- Make sure you're aware of any restrictions placed by the platform itself - some platforms don't approve certain images or content, so it's important to check ahead of time before launching any campaigns.

Creating an advertising budget is also essential for freelance writers looking to invest in paid media platforms. It's important to remember that your budget does not have to be large but should allow enough flexibility for experimentation and testing. Start by assessing what kind of return on investment you want from your campaign, then allocate funds accordingly. If you don't have a lot of money, it may be best to start with smaller campaigns first or focus on one platform at a time with limited exposure until you are confident in success rates before expanding further.

An example of an advertising budget a freelancer could use would depend on the size and scope of their business and their available resources. For instance, you might allocate 10% of gross revenue to marketing to ensure consistent growth. This will allow for some experimentation and testing when launching new campaigns while still covering day-to-day operations.

When calculating potential returns from advertising, it is important to focus on key performance indicators (KPIs) that show performance relative to your objectives. The average cost per click (CPC) or cost per acquisition (CPA) are two metrics that can help determine how much you spend to acquire customers from paid media platforms. Additionally, customer lifetime value (CLV) can be calculated to measure a customer's overall profitability over their entire lifespan. CLV can provide great insight into your ads' effectiveness in achieving successful ROI for your business.

Crafting Unique Ad Copy & Specialized Funnels for Maximum Conversion Rate

Crafting unique ad copy and specialized funnels is essential to optimize advertising campaigns and maximize conversion rates. With the right combination of creative copy and targeted messaging, you can make sure your advertising reaches the right people and entices them to become customers.

When creating ad copy, it's important to keep it simple and direct. This could include a simple call-to-action like "Sign up now!" or a hook that appeals to the target audience, like "Unlock exclusive discounts with our rewards program." The goal should be to create an eye-catching headline that stands out among all other ads while still conveying a clear message in only a few words. You should also include visuals in your ads as this help draw attention and build interest for potential customers.

Specialized funnels are a critical component of successful online marketing campaigns. They allow businesses to break down complex customer journeys into smaller steps (or stages), making it easier for customers to move through the process without getting overwhelmed. A specialized funnel might look something like this:

- Awareness
- Interest
- Evaluation
- Purchase Decision
- Conversion

Each "stage" of the funnel would have its own tasks to convert leads into sales, such as providing content offers in each stage or running promotional campaigns targeting users based on their engagement level in previous stages. By focusing on maximizing conversion rates within each stage of the funnel, businesses can significantly increase their return on investment from paid media platforms.

The combination of unique ad copy and specialized funnels are powerful tools that every freelance writer should consider utilizing when crafting marketing strategies to continually drive success within their business operations. By understanding which tactics work best for your goals, you can craft effectively designed campaigns that convert viewers into loyal customers.

By the way, for freelance writers looking to specialize in advertising, writing ad copy and funnels can be a great niche to explore. Not only does this allow writers to hone their creative skills and develop an understanding of marketing principles, but it also gives them a chance to sharpen their ability to analyze customer behavior and craft effective messages that convert leads into sales. By leveraging their writing talents and understanding of consumer psychology, freelance writers can create messaging that resonates with target audiences and helps drive meaningful results for businesses.

Developing Structured Content Strategies for Long-Term Growth

If you're a freelancer looking to grow your business and reach new audiences, developing structured content strategies is essential. However, your content must be well thought out and planned in advance to ensure long-term success. This involves implementing an editorial calendar or discovery document and repurposing content into different formats, such as ebooks, podcasts, and video tutorials. This section will discuss why these two approaches are necessary for structuring successful content strategies for long-term growth and increased revenues for freelancers.

Implementing an Editorial Calendar or Discovery Doc to Plan Content in Advance

An editorial calendar or discovery doc is used to plan content. This document will provide a roadmap, detailing topics and deadlines that should be adhered to in order to ensure content output is consistent, timely and organized. By providing clear instructions on when and what content should be written, an editorial calendar or discovery doc makes it easier to manage workloads more efficiently.

When planning content using an editorial calendar or discovery doc, there are some best practices to adhere to:

- Start by setting realistic goals based on your available time and what type of content you want to create (i.e., blog posts, videos, webinars).
- Include deadlines for each piece and milestones so you can track your progress as you go along.
- Break up complex topics into smaller chunks to tackle them one at a time and complete your work faster.

By understanding the concept behind an editorial calendar or discovery doc and following these best practices when creating one, you can ensure that your content strategies are structured for long-term growth. Doing so helps you build an engaged readership base that keeps returning for more.

Repurposing Content into Different Formats (eBooks, Podcasts, Video Tutorials)

Repurposing content for different formats is a great way to maximize your reach and generate additional revenue streams. Creating one piece of content and then reshaping, condensing, or expanding that content into multiple formats allows you to produce engaging pieces that appeal to a wider range of readers and listeners.

For example, a multiple blog posts on similar topics or keywords can be easily repurposed into an ebook, podcast episode, or video tutorial with few modifications. You could also turn a single blog post into an ebook by adding more detailed information. Or you could use the voice recording app on your phone to record and transcribe an audio version of the same piece to create a podcast episode. Similarly, you could record yourself narrating the post to be used as a video tutorial.

Repurposing content also has the potential to increase offers for sponsorships or other partnerships which can contribute additional revenue streams for freelance writers. For instance, if you've created an ebook from your blog post, you could offer sponsorships towards this product in return for a fee. Additionally, if you were using your podcast as part of an affiliate program, each listener who purchases the program would generate additional incremental income.

By planning ahead and creating content with repurposing in mind, freelance writers can leverage their work to create useful products or services that are both cost-effective and time-saving in the long run. To do this, consider which format best suits your topic before writing.

For instance, if you want to create something visual, then think about whether it would be better suited as an infographic or motion graphic video. After you decide, write accordingly so that less editing is required during the repurposing process. Once the piece is complete, promote it across all platforms – including social media – and remember to include links back to where people can find your original material too.

Exploring Different Freelance Writing Business Models

Starting a successful freelance writing business requires a deep understanding of the existing business models and how to best capitalize on them. This section will discuss how to research other writers and fee structures, set different rates for various types of work (e.g. copywriting vs content writing), and develop specialized services or create niche offers to target specific industries for maximum impact.

When researching other writers and fee structures, a market analysis is key. Consider the rate for similar services or articles and decide accordingly, remembering it's important to stand out amongst the competition. Additionally, take into account the scope of work and quality requirements to calculate competitive rates while still producing quality output. Setting different rates for different types of work is also essential, as copywriting may require different expertise than content writing yet have similar market value. Lastly, developing niche specialty services can be beneficial when targeting certain industries. These could include technical writing or creating informative reports on specific topics. With these methods in mind, you'll be well-prepared to build a successful and profitable freelance writing business.

Researching Other Writers & Exploring Various Fee Structures

Researching other writers can be crucial in deciding on the right fee structure for your freelance writing business. A good way to begin researching other writers is to look up their professional profiles and reviews, so you can gain insight into their style of writing and how they handle different projects.

Additionally, you can use market analysis to compare related services and get a sense of what the rate should be. For example, content writing focuses more on providing informative, valuable information to readers that is interesting and well-researched. Therefore, copywriters may be able to charge higher rates due to their specialized skill set, even though they are both in the same industry. Lastly, developing niche specialty services can be beneficial when targeting certain industries; this could include technical writing or creating informative reports on specific topics.

When it comes to exploring fee structures for freelance writing services, there are several key models to consider:

- Flat fees can be offered as one-time payments for projects of every type and size. These deals are great for clients who need assurance that their project is completed within budget and

timeframe but may not work well for larger projects where specific deliverables require more detailed negotiation.
- Hourly billing is an excellent way for clients to ensure they will receive precisely the metric of service they have requested, but it may not be the most cost-effective option due to time clock optimization concerns.
- Pay per word is another option. It provides predictable pricing while allowing freelancers some autonomy over the task.
- Retainer agreements offer a greater measure of security and stability to both parties. Related tasks can often be accomplished in bulk at these times rather than having separate communications each time a task arises.

Setting Different Rates for Different Types of Work

It is important to set different rates for different types of work to ensure that you are properly compensated and that your client gets the best value for their money. Copywriting and content writing require two distinct sets of skills and should not be lumped together when setting rates. For copywriting, writers need to bring an eye for detail and creativity, while content writers must have a deep understanding of the subject matter they are covering. As such, each type of writing deserves its own rate.

In addition to copywriting and content writing, there are a variety of other freelance jobs that may require different billing rates. For example, crafting compelling headlines or designing eye-catching visuals for blog posts and articles can involve significant time spent on concept creation, research and multiple revisions. Similarly, proofreading and editing services necessitate more intensive project management to keep everything moving smoothly. Additionally, researching topics to create an insightful case study or developing an engaging newsletter template involves a set of unique skill sets that can merit varying compensation levels accordingly.

When talking to clients about different rates for different types of work, it helps to explain what is involved in each project so they understand why there are separate charges. Knowing which areas require more time and effort can help explain the price tag attached to each job without putting the client off with a seemingly arbitrary number. It also builds trust between both parties by showing that you have taken the time to put together a fair and accurate quote based on their individual needs.

For a freelance writer looking to set competitive rates, market research can be extremely helpful in determining a fair price point for each project. Evaluating similar services or articles on the market and evaluating them is one way to get an idea of how much other writers charge for certain types of content or tasks. Additionally, having a dedicated portfolio page with past projects or samples can assist potential clients in making an informed decision about hiring you and provide justification for rates should those questions arise during negotiations.

Developing Specialty Services or Creating Niche Offers To Target Specific Industries

Competition is fierce in the freelance writing business and it can be tough to stand out among the dozens of other talented professionals vying for the same gigs. One way to differentiate yourself is by offering specialty services or creating niche offers to target specific industries.

When you offer specialty services or work in highly sought-after sub-niches, you distinguish yourself from other freelancers providing a more general service. This helps make you more visible to potential clients and makes it easier for them to find you when searching for someone with your specific skillset. It also shows that you have expertise in an area that others may not possess—making your services more valuable than your competition. Additionally, when you offer specialty services or create niche offers, clients will likely view you as an expert who understands their needs—making them more likely to hire you.

Niche offers can also help increase your visibility and customer base. For example, suppose you offer website copywriting services and specialize in writing content for the fashion industry. In that case, potential clients looking for someone with experience in the fashion industry can easily find and contact you when they search online. Offering niche services like this increases the chances of being hired by companies or individuals looking for someone with specific knowledge or expertise in a certain area. Additionally, this approach allows you to focus on building relationships within that particular industry—which can lead to additional opportunities down the line.

Another advantage of offering specialty services or creating niche offers is that it allows you to build your brand as a freelance writer even more effectively than before. When clients see that there is something unique about what you do—such as targeting specific industries—they are going to remember that about your business and will be more likely to recommend your services (or hire you again) if they need something similar in the future. And since word-of-mouth recommendations are one of the most powerful forms of marketing, having people spread positive things about what your business does can be invaluable when it comes time to acquire new clients.

Chapter 13 You're Not Superhuman: How to Maintain a Healthy Work/Life Balance

As a freelance writer, you're constantly balancing the demands of your work and personal life. You must juggle multiple projects simultaneously, manage deadlines, and still find time for yourself. It's an amazing but challenging lifestyle. In this chapter, we'll discuss why it's essential for writers to maintain a healthy balance between their professional and personal lives – and how to successfully do so without burning out. We'll look at strategies for avoiding burnout, knowing your limitations, setting boundaries, reducing distractions with technology, utilizing available resources and more.

Why Maintaining Work/Life Balance Is Essential for Freelance Writers

As a freelance writer, creating a healthy work-life balance is essential for your well-being and overall success. The freedom of working from home or on the go can make it difficult to draw a clear line between work and your personal life, leading to out-of-control workloads and exhaustion. If you don't maintain your work/life balance, you may find yourself feeling overwhelmed, overworked, and unmotivated to create your best work.

By understanding the importance of maintaining a balance between professional endeavors and self-care, you can become more productive in less time without sacrificing yourself. Setting boundaries around when to stop working can help keep you focused while ensuring you have time for yourself. Regular breaks throughout the day allow your mind to process what you've been doing while giving your body much-needed rest. You should also look into finding resources like co-working spaces or networks that can provide new opportunities and inspiration without monopolizing all of your waking hours.

With powerful planning tools and an understanding of why it's essential to prioritize both work and personal life, you are sure to get the most out of freelance writing while keeping burnout at bay. Creating achievable goals to boost motivation and employing supportive measures such as therapy or yoga can help you stay balanced and more productive. Don't forget to reward yourself after completing tasks, be it taking a holiday or simply treating yourself to something special! Making sure you take care of your whole self is one of the best ways for freelance writers to remain successful in their careers.

Knowing Your Limitations and Setting Boundaries

No matter how hard we try, it's impossible to do everything. Knowing your limitations and setting boundaries is vital to ensure that you can maintain a healthy balance between work and personal life. Setting clear limits around expectations, activities and commitments will help prevent you from becoming overwhelmed while ensuring that you prioritize existing commitments before taking on new ones.

Limiting distractions can also help keep focus on what's important, such as not responding to emails or notifications outside of pre-defined office hours. Prioritizing sleep and self-care practices such as exercise, healthy eating, and taking breaks throughout the day will further help you stay productive without sacrificing yourself. Additionally, freelancers need to remember that if a project isn't feasible due to time or other constraints, then communicating this with employers/clients is essential, both for your own well-being and trustworthiness.

Having a good understanding of your capabilities can also help build an efficient workflow that allows you to make the most of available resources while still staying within what's manageable and sustainable for you. Keep track of time spent on projects, invest in tools that make prioritizing tasks easier, or consider outsourcing certain elements of work if feasible so as not to overextend yourself past a certain point. Even though it can be difficult at times, knowing your limitations and setting boundaries is an important part of staying mentally healthy yet still being successful in freelance writing.

Strategies for Avoiding Burnout as a Freelancer

The temptation to take on too much work in this business and ignore your own boundaries can be great. That's why it is essential that you understand the potential for burnout and have strategies in place to help you avoid it. Here are some tips on how to prevent burnout as a freelancer:

1. Set Boundaries: It's important to set boundaries between work time and personal life. This means limiting when you will respond to emails or notifications, and taking breaks during the day. It also means creating achievable goals, so you're not trying to do too much at once.

2. Prioritize Self-Care: Make sure you take care of yourself both physically and mentally by getting enough sleep, eating healthy, exercising regularly, and engaging in activities that bring joy into your life.

3. Take Breaks During The Day: Regular breaks throughout the day allow your mind and body to rest from their efforts while allowing you to reset and refocus before continuing work. Breaks can include short walks, listening to music, or just taking a few minutes away from your computer screen.

4. Create A Support System: Having reliable people who understand what it's like being a freelancer can make all the difference when feeling

overwhelmed or burnt out. Whether finding co-working spaces or joining groups related to your field, connecting with others in similar positions will provide new opportunities and valuable support networks that cannot be found elsewhere.

Balancing Your Workload on Multiple Projects

For the freelancer, managing your workload can be an uphill battle. With multiple projects going on at once, it can be difficult to remain organized and productive. Unfortunately, this often leads to burnout and fatigue from too many commitments. To avoid this, freelance writers must learn how to balance their workload effectively by following some simple strategies. This will help them stay focused and productive while avoiding becoming overwhelmed by the work they have taken on.

Here are some tips on how to balance multiple projects:

1. Set Priorities: Make a list of all current assignments and prioritize them in order of importance so that you can focus your energy where it is needed most.

Setting priorities is essential to use your time and energy effectively. Make a list of all the assignments you must complete in order of importance so that you can focus on the most important tasks first. It's important to note that some tasks may require more resources or take longer to finish than others, so it's important to allocate accordingly.

Certain tasks may have set deadlines or require teamwork with other people, which should influence how you prioritize. Additionally, if a task requires multiple steps, breaking it into smaller segments will make it easier to manage and track progress toward completion. Prioritizing your tasks allows you to work smarter and stay focused on what matters most for successfully completing your projects.

2. Keep a Schedule: An organized schedule helps track tasks and deadlines while also allowing you to plan ahead for upcoming assignments. Scheduling out the day or week in advance ensures you don't fall behind or become overwhelmed by last-minute requests.

Having a structured schedule is a great way to ensure you stay on top of tasks and meet all deadlines. First, figure out what tasks need to be done for the day or week and prioritize them in order of importance. This will help you plan your time accordingly and keep track of how much time each task requires. Set clear objectives for each day so you know when each task should be completed. When working with teams, try to coordinate schedules so you can divide responsibilities appropriately and have enough time to get everything done.

3. Break Up Projects Into Smaller Tasks: Breaking up projects into smaller, more manageable tasks not only makes the workload easier to manage but also allows each task to be worked on individually and thus avoid feeling overwhelmed by the entire project.

Start by making a list of all the necessary steps for the project, so you have a clear idea of what needs to be done. Then, identify which tasks are most important and allocate time accordingly. Longer-term tasks should be broken down into shorter ones, while shorter tasks can be combined to save time. Working on each task individually will help you stay focused and motivated as you progress toward completing the project. It's also important to track your progress so that you can adjust your timeline if needed and make sure everything is completed on time.

4. Delegate When Necessary: If you find yourself overburdened with too many commitments, consider outsourcing certain work elements or delegating responsibilities to colleagues or VAs who might help relieve some stress from the workload.

Delegating responsibilities is a great way to reduce the workload and ensure all tasks are completed on time. Consider which tasks are most important and prioritize them accordingly. Those tasks that don't require your expertise or knowledge can be delegated so that you can focus on other areas of work. When delegating work, it's important to provide clear verbal and written instructions so that everyone knows what they have to do.

Additionally, it's best to set deadlines and follow-up meetings with the person completing the task so that you can be sure it is done correctly and on schedule. Finally, remember that delegating does not mean abdicating – you should still stay involved and provide guidance when necessary. By delegating certain elements of work, you can help ensure that everything gets done on time without feeling overwhelmed or overburdened with too many commitments.

Balancing Your Workload as a Writer: Strategies for Staying Energized and Productive

As a freelance writer, managing your workload can be challenging. Juggling multiple projects and commitments can quickly lead to burnout and fatigue, so staying organized and productive is essential.

- To do this, start by assessing all of your current commitments. Work out how much time you need for each task and prioritize the most urgent projects. This will help ensure you're on track with your writing targets and free up time for other tasks.
- Organization is key when it comes to staying productive as a writer. Create a detailed work schedule that includes deadlines and goals for each project, allowing yourself extra time in case of any unexpected delays or disruptions. Keep everything in one place so you can easily access any materials

- or information related to each piece of writing.
- When things get too much, take breaks or move on to something else if that helps clear your mind and reset your focus. While keeping up with deadlines is important, allowing yourself some downtime is just as necessary for maintaining productivity levels over the long term. You don't want to end up burnt out because you spread yourself too thin!
- Finally, ensure you have an effective support network when things get tough. Having someone who can offer advice or act as an accountability partner could make a big difference in keeping your motivation levels consistent.

Taking Breaks and Scheduling Time for Yourself Without Feeling Guilty About It

Taking breaks and scheduling time for yourself are essential for maintaining productivity, especially in a hectic job like freelance writing. Many writers feel guilty when they take time off, but doing so is actually beneficial in the long run. Regular breaks allow you to recharge and reset your focus, meaning you'll be more productive when you return to work.

When scheduling break times, plan ahead and set realistic goals. Make sure that you stick to this schedule – don't let work commitments creep in when it's your designated break. Take advantage of any allocated off days by taking a break from technology or going for a walk – any activity that helps clear your mind and replenish your energy levels.

It's also important to recognize signs of stress and fatigue before they escalate further.

Signs of personal stress or fatigue for a freelancer to watch out for include difficulty focusing, procrastination, feeling overwhelmed, difficulty sleeping, and irritability. If you start to notice these signs in yourself, it may be time to take a break and relax. Take the time to do something that makes you happy – maybe read a book or take a walk – whatever helps restore your energy levels.

If it feels like too much or if your workload is becoming overwhelming, reduce your hours or take some extra time off if you can afford to do so. Remember that time away from work can ultimately help instead of hinder progress. Finally, make sure that the breaks you take are worthwhile. Find activities that bring joy or happiness, such as spending quality time with family or friends or venturing outside your comfort zone and trying something new. When these practices become part of your regular routine, being productive without feeling guilty will be much easier.

How To Recognize When You're Getting Overwhelmed and How To Get Back on Track Quickly

Feeling overwhelmed can be a common occurrence for freelance writers. Recognizing when it's happening is key to staying on top of your workload and avoiding burnout.

The most obvious signs of feeling overwhelmed are a sense of overwhelm, anxiety or depression, fatigue, difficulty concentrating, lack of motivation and even physical aches or pains. If any of these symptoms manifest during your workday, take time away from your writing desk and assess what's causing the stress.

When you feel overwhelmed, it's important to remain calm and make sure that you don't try to do too much in too short a timeframe. You may want to take some time off or reduce your workload if possible; this could help clear your mind and reset your focus. Regular breaks throughout the day also prevent further stress and fatigue from building up over time.

In addition, make sure you have an effective support system for times like these – reaching out for help or advice from friends or colleagues can often help put things into perspective quickly. Finally, review your goals so that they are achievable within the given timeframe; having clearly defined expectations will help keep motivation levels high even when challenges arise

Using Technology Wisely While Writing – Minimizing Distractions and Maximizing Productivity

Technology can be both a blessing and a curse in writing. On the one hand, it can provide abundant resources and tools for research and creativity. But on the other hand, it can be a major distraction from actually completing tasks. It is important to use technology wisely, being mindful of its potential benefits and pitfalls. Here are some tips for minimizing distractions and maximizing productivity when using technology for writing:

1. Establish clear goals and timelines – Set achievable goals with realistic deadlines before starting a project. This will help keep you motivated to work towards completion while avoiding taking on too much in too little time.

Establishing clear goals and timelines is essential for any project. It's important to ask yourself, "What are my objectives?" and then set realistic deadlines that won't jeopardize your overall timeline. Breaking up your tasks into smaller chunks will help you stay on track and make steady progress toward completion. Additionally, setting goals gives you something tangible to strive for. They provide a sense of purpose, focus your energy, and enable you to measure success.

When creating a timeline, try to be as realistic as possible about how long it will take to complete each task. Doing so ensures that nothing gets lost in the shuffle. Finally, don't hesitate to seek help if needed. Delegate parts of the work or ask for advice from colleagues with similar project experience. By taking some time upfront to plan and set achievable goals (with realistic timelines) you can ensure that each project is completed on time and meets its desired objectives.

2. Turn off notifications – Audio or visual alerts can take your mind off what you're doing, so disable these notifications while working on your project.

Turning off notifications is a great way to stay focused on your project and avoid distraction. Notifications are designed to grab your attention and disrupt the workflow, removing focus from the task. Turning off audio and visual alerts eliminates distractions that may prevent you from completing your work on time. Before starting work on any project, take a few minutes to disable notifications from your email, social media accounts, or other apps that could potentially pull you away.

Additionally, take advantage of "do not disturb" settings available on many devices - this can help ensure that nothing will interrupt you for as long as needed so that you can stay focused on your work. Finally, consider utilizing a time-blocking system where you designate specific times during the day for tasks - this will help keep both mind and body energized while moving the project forward without interruption. By disabling all potential distractions before starting work on any project, you can remain undisturbed so that all of your goals are efficiently achieved.

3. Use a focusing app – Apps like Focus Keeper or Freedom can block out distracting websites while allowing access to necessary research sites.

A focusing app can be extremely beneficial when working on any project or task. Focus Keeper and Freedom are two popular apps that allow you to create an "internet bubble," blocking out all unnecessary websites while allowing access to the research sites you need to do the job. It's important to note that this type of app is not only intended for use during work or personal hours – it can also be used when taking a break from productivity. This helps prevent unhealthy internet habits such as procrastination or spending too much time on social media. Additionally, these apps allow you to set custom web blocks and alerts so that you know exactly how much time you're dedicating to certain tasks.

4. Break down tasks into smaller chunks – Breaking big projects into smaller sections that require shorter completion times is beneficial in keeping focus levels high and preventing overwhelming feelings from setting in.

First, create a list of the steps needed to complete the project. Then prioritize which tasks are most important and assign deadlines to each one to set yourself up for motivation and success. Working this way allows you to focus on one task at a time, giving you a sense of accomplishment each time you cross one off your list.

Additionally, breaking down tasks into smaller chunks allows you to pause or take a break between sections as needed to stay clear-headed throughout the project's completion. Finally, multiple due dates can help keep your momentum going while ensuring everything gets done without feeling rushed or overwhelmed. Breaking down projects into small chunks is essential for maintaining focus and managing the work efficiently so that all goals are easily met.

Maintaining a Healthy Work/Life Balance as a Freelance Writer

As a freelance writer, you're constantly juggling the demands of your work and personal life. Managing multiple projects simultaneously, meeting deadlines, and still finding time for yourself can be challenging. However, it's essential to maintain a healthy balance between your professional and personal life to avoid burnout and achieve long-term success.

To maintain a healthy work/life balance, consider the following strategies:

- Know your limitations and set realistic goals to avoid overworking yourself or taking on more than you can handle.
- Prioritize self-care activities such as exercise, meditation, or engaging in a hobby to recharge your batteries and reduce stress.
- Set boundaries for your work schedule, so you know when to stop working and begin focusing on your personal life.
- Utilize available resources and tools to increase productivity and reduce distractions, such as time-tracking apps or website blockers.
- Avoid multitasking and focus on one task at a time to increase productivity and reduce the risk of burnout.

Implementing these strategies can help you maintain a healthy balance between your work and personal life, leading to increased satisfaction and success in your freelance writing career.

Remember, you're not superhuman, and maintaining a healthy balance is essential to avoid burnout and achieve long-term success. By prioritizing self-care, setting boundaries, and focusing on one task at a time, you can maintain high levels of productivity while enjoying a fulfilling personal life.

Chapter 14 Diversifying Your Income: Why It's Important and How to Do It

John and Emily are two successful freelance content creators. John has been in the game for years and relies heavily on two main clients for his income. Things have been going well, and John has not felt the need to search for new clients or income streams beyond his two dependable sources. He has coasted along, thinking that he has enough work to get by, so why bother expanding his client base or exploring new income opportunities?

Meanwhile, Emily, relatively new to the freelance scene, has intentionally pursued multiple income streams, from social media management to web copywriting to e-book ghostwriting. She maintains consistent income from all these sources, not relying on any one specific client or project entirely.

Fast forward a year. John's primary client decides to cut back on their content needs, and he loses nearly 50% of his income. The other client has a shift in priorities and decides to allocate funds elsewhere. As a result, John finds himself with a drastic reduction in income and no other clients to turn to.

Emily, on the other hand, experiences no significant loss of income because she has created a diversified income stream through her various writing services. In fact, her steady income has allowed her to take on more interesting projects, such as writing for a magazine, something she had always wanted to do.

The lesson here is that diversifying your income streams is crucial to success as a freelance content creator. Relying too heavily on one client, project, or income stream can lead to financial instability and ultimately harm your career. By intentionally creating multiple sources of income, you can build a buffer against the unpredictable nature of freelancing, find new and exciting projects, and ultimately increase your earning potential.

In the following chapter, we'll explore several strategies for diversifying your income as a freelancer.

Why Income Diversification Matters

Income diversification is essential for freelance writers who are looking to achieve financial success. That's because things can be going along perfectly fine until they come to a screeching halt, as they did in John's case. By having multiple income streams, freelance writers can better protect themselves against potential fluctuations in the market, unexpected downturns and industry changes, as well as personal financial problems like medical bills or job loss. A diversified income portfolio can also help writers maximize their earning potential and take advantage of multiple opportunities.

One example of how diversifying income can benefit freelance writers is minimizing risk. For instance, if a writer only has one source of income, such as writing articles for a single client, they are more vulnerable to changes in the market that could affect their total earnings. However, suppose that same writer diversifies their income to include other sources with different levels of risk, such as setting up their own blog or creating digital products and services. In that case, they can spread the risk across multiple sources and potentially earn more money overall.

Another benefit of income diversification is that it encourages creativity and innovation. Having multiple income streams allows you to explore different ways to monetize your skills and create new opportunities. For example, by offering additional services like podcasting or teaching workshops on how to become a successful freelancer on top of providing written content, you can increase your revenue while building an audience at the same time.

Income diversification also gives freelance writers flexibility regarding when and where they work. With multiple sources of income coming from different areas, they can choose which projects they want to focus on depending on what works best for them regarding both time and money investments. This allows them to enjoy some freedom and feel less tied down when it comes to work commitments while still reaping the benefits financially.

The Risks of Not Diversifying Your Income Streams

When freelancers rely solely on a single source of income, they are putting themselves at major risk of experiencing financial loss. A freelance writer who only sells their content to one client is particularly vulnerable to potential market fluctuations. If the demand for the type of content they produce unexpectedly drops off, this could cause them to lose a large portion of their income. Unexpected industry changes can also dampen earnings. For example, if new regulations limit or restrict the types of writing a freelance writer can do, then not having other income streams can make it difficult to weather these unexpected downturns.

Some regulations affecting freelance writers include copyright laws, intellectual property rights, censorship rules, and national security laws. These regulations could limit what topics a writer can write about, restrict where they can publish their work, or impose certain restrictions on how certain types of content are shared. Additionally, some countries may have language-based restrictions prohibiting certain subjects from being discussed in writing.

Financial problems from medical bills or job loss can also be daunting to deal with when there is just one source of income. Without any additional help from another form of income, freelancers in these circumstances may find it hard to stay afloat and take longer to get back on track than usual.

In addition to the issues above, not diversifying income also carries psychological risks. When freelance writers rely solely on one source, they may feel stuck or become complacent instead of motivated – leading them to feel weighed down by work and distracted from completing tasks due to their lack of options. This kind of stagnation in an otherwise dynamic career path can take away the joys associated with freelancing and potentially breed resentment toward the profession altogether.

Maximizing Earning Potential

As a freelance writer, there are numerous opportunities to increase your earning potential in the current market. By taking advantage of the right approach and techniques, you can establish multiple sources of income and manage risk effectively.

One key to maximizing earnings is to leverage existing talents and opportunities. Researching markets to determine where freelance talents are in demand and taking on assignments that best suit your skillsets and interests is essential. Making the most of existing contacts or networks can also help you find new and exciting opportunities.

Another way to increase your earning potential is through diversification. Avoid over-reliance on any particular source of income by creating multiple streams of revenue. This can mean exploring new writing niches, branching out to different types of clients, or developing new skills that complement your existing ones.

Effective risk management is also essential for long-term profitability. Setting limits on workloads or expenses when necessary can help protect profit margins. Continuously researching for new opportunities and staying ahead of industry trends also helps.

How to Create Multiple Streams of Income

Exploring new opportunities and freelancing fields can be a great way to create multiple income streams. Consider researching the markets to determine which areas are in demand and what skillsets are needed to maximize your talents and interests. Building a portfolio and getting referrals is also essential—it will enable you to demonstrate your qualifications and help spread awareness of your services. Furthermore, leveraging new technologies and techniques will allow you to maximize your income potential. Social media platforms, for example, offer an excellent avenue for connecting with potential employers or clients and staying updated on industry news.

Freelancing is an excellent way for writers to find new opportunities and explore new fields. With the increasing rise of the gig economy, more people than ever are turning to freelancing for the flexibility it offers. From marketing and copywriting to podcasting and travel writing, there are a plethora of possibilities for anyone looking to break into freelance work.

In addition to exploring existing fields, freelancers can also develop unique services and products. Whether it's a special brand of writing or a particular area of specialization, having something different in your arsenal can make you stand out from the crowd and land more long-term projects with clients. Even if you're already an established writer, you can continually challenge yourself by honing new skills or taking on complex projects. The benefits of pursuing new opportunities may not be immediately apparent, but they often result in incredible professional growth that could open even more rewarding doors down the road.

Building a portfolio is one of the most important steps in succeeding as a freelancer. Collecting work samples and showcasing your talents to potential clients can help you stand out and land more jobs. To build a portfolio, start by creating a website that highlights your writing skills and experience. Make sure it is easy to navigate and has contact information clearly visible. Additionally, using social media channels such as Twitter or LinkedIn can be an effective way to advertise yourself as a writer and network with fellow freelancers.

Getting referrals from other writers or businesses you've worked for is also key when trying to break into freelancing. Ask former employers if they'd be willing to provide a professional reference for you or mention your services on their website or social media platforms. Word-of-mouth advertising can be powerful because it increases the trustworthiness of your business in the eyes of potential clients.

Utilizing new technologies and techniques can be a great way for to maximize your income. For example, marketing automation tools can help you identify potential leads and connect with them quickly and easily. Additionally, leveraging social media platforms allows writers to reach a larger audience and increase their chances of getting hired for writing gigs. Utilizing SEO copywriting techniques will also help optimize content for search engines, increasing their visibility online. Finally, using project management software helps writers stay organized, resulting in more efficient workflows.

Leveraging Existing Talents and Opportunities

As a freelance writer, leveraging existing talents and opportunities is a great way to diversify your income streams. By finding work that complements your existing skills and interests, you can create multiple sources of income that will provide financial stability and long-term success.

One way to leverage your talents is to research the markets where freelance writing skills are most in demand. Consider niches in which you have a particular interest or expertise, such as technology, healthcare, or finance. Identify the needs and desires of clients in these niches and adjust your service offerings to meet these needs. This will help you become specialized in your niche and will allow you to charge a premium for your services.

Another way to leverage existing talents is to take on assignments or projects that complement your current offerings. For example, if you are a skilled writer, you may consider taking on related roles such as editing, proofreading or content management. By offering services beyond just writing, you can build a broader range of services that will help you attract more clients and increase your earning potential.

An alternate approach is to focus on the types of projects that you enjoy the most. If you already have a particular writing skillset, consider expanding upon that skillset by taking classes, workshops or certificates so that you can take on more specialized and higher paying projects. This can lead to higher rates per project and ultimately lead to a more fulfilling career.

Taking advantage of these opportunities will expand your skillset and help you create multiple sources of revenue. By using your talents and exploring new opportunities, you can establish a more stable financial foothold in the competitive field of freelance writing.

Making the most of existing contacts and networks is also essential to being a successful freelancer. An extended network can open up new opportunities, provide insights into particular sectors or industries, and help you stay on track with industry trends. To start with, it's important to reach out to current contacts and reconnect with former colleagues – communicate your freelance goals and ask them for references or advice. Additionally, join relevant professional groups or follow people on social media who can offer valuable guidance and expertise.

Once your network is established, don't forget to nurture it: keep them updated on any milestones and successes and highlight any struggles or obstacles you face so they know how they can help and support you. Additionally, don't limit yourself to only contacting friends or colleagues. Think outside the box: look into mentorships or manage projects within public sector organizations that could add more depth to your portfolio.

Finally, use your connections as resources – review job postings from other professionals in the field, read up on their experiences working as freelancers in that industry, and ask for feedback about project ideas or new business models. Making the most of existing contacts and networks takes dedication, but it can be extremely beneficial when looking for project opportunities or navigating certain market sectors.

Effectively Managing Risk

Effectively managing risk is a key part of being a successful freelance writer. One way to reduce risk is to diversify income sources by taking on projects from different industries or clients and utilizing income streams such as passive income. This practice helps to avoid over-relying on any particular source of income and gives the freelancer more control over their financial situation.

Another way to manage risk is to set limits on workloads or expenses when necessary to protect profit margins. For instance, consider setting realistic deadlines that allow you enough time without sacrificing quality, or only take projects with payment amounts that cover all your costs, plus a fair rate for your services. Similarly, don't forget about budgeting for contingencies such as emergency health care costs or unexpected tax payments so that you can keep operating without delays or problems if something unexpected arises.

In addition, make sure you have documentation and agreements in place regarding the scope and timeline of each project, fees due and other details related to the work. These documents can protect both the client and the freelancer from any misunderstandings down the line. With proactive risk management strategies like these, freelance writers can feel more secure in their work environment while still reaching their professional goals.

Another option is to look into alternative markets, such as international freelance opportunities or online marketplaces with higher demand for certain skill sets. Freelancers can also expand their service offerings beyond writing and explore related fields such as podcasting, website building, or offering virtual assistant services. Taking advantage of these expanding markets can help broaden the range of income sources while still allowing you to use your existing writing skills.

Finally, don't forget about creating residual sources of revenue, such as books or e-courses, which offer a reliable stream of passive recurring income. By diversifying your income sources and exploring different niches and markets, you can protect yourself against sudden changes in the industry and keep your business flexible enough to adapt when necessary.

20 Ideas To Help Diversify a Writer's Income

Diversifying your income as a freelance writer is essential to maintaining financial stability, especially in an ever-changing market. By exploring different revenue streams, you can develop new skills, offer more services to clients, and increase your earning potential. This can help bring security in times of uncertainty and provide a cushion to cushion any unexpected downturns.

Here are some ideas to help you broaden your portfolio:

1. Offer Social Media Management Services: Social media services are in high demand, particularly by small to medium-sized businesses that require professional management of their digital presence. You can offer services such as creating and scheduling posts and running ads.

2. Write Product Descriptions for eCommerce Sites: eCommerce sites like Amazon require descriptive content for their products. You can offer services to write these descriptions, enhancing the shopper's experience and helping sellers to make more sales.

3. Write Content for Blogs: Many businesses maintain blogs to help support their brand image and create awareness for their products or services. You can leverage this opportunity by offering to write content for their blogs.

4. Offer eBook Writing: eBooks are an excellent resource for businesses looking to showcase their expertise or expand their brand visibility. Consider offering eBook writing services to businesses in your niche.

5. Create Email Campaigns: Email campaigns remain an essential component of digital marketing efforts, and businesses require quality content for email campaigns. You can offer services such as writing subject lines, creating copy, and developing email campaigns schedules.

6. Offer Copywriting Services: Copywriting services are in high demand in industries such as marketing, advertising, and even public relations. Offer these services to businesses and help them bolster catchy copy for their advertisements and PR efforts.

7. Write Resume and Cover Letter Writing: Many people need assistance when it comes to creating a compelling resume or cover letter to win that first job interview. This can be an opportunity to create a thriving service offering.

8. Write Grant Proposals: Government agencies and non-profit organizations require grant proposals to secure funding for their programs. Helping these organizations can be a lucrative way to diversify your writing portfolio.

9. Offer Press Release Services: Press releases are a way for businesses to gain exposure in various media channels. Offer services to maximize visibility and keep effective communication with their target audience.

10. Create White Papers for Businesses: White papers are an excellent way to showcase expertise in a particular industry. You can offer white paper writing services to businesses looking to establish themselves as thought leaders in their fields.

11. Write for Newsletters: Companies often produce newsletters as a way to connect with their audiences regularly. Provide quality content to businesses to help set them apart.

12. Offer Technical Writing Services: Technical writing can be immensely challenging, and businesses are often in need of professionals to help them with manuals, guides, and other technical documents.

13. Write Reviews: You can monetize content creation by providing written reviews of products, services, or even books. You can offer a perspective that resonates with your target audience.

14. Contribute to Industry Magazines: Many magazines are happy to receive contributed content from freelance writers. Identify

publications in your chosen niche and offer contributing content and develop relationships.

15. Create Video Scripts: As video content becomes increasingly important, the demand for well-written scripts increases. You can offer video scriptwriting services to businesses that seek more engagement on social media sites such as YouTube, Twitch, and more.

16. Offer Party Scriptwriting Services: Party scripts are a fun and creative way to celebrate birthdays, anniversaries and more. You can offer to write personalized scripts for themed parties, weddings, and other events.

17. Ghostwrite for Social Media Influencers: Social media influencers often need assistance in crafting posts or writing captions in their brand's voice. Offer your writing services to help them get their message across to their large audiences.

18. Write for Children's Books: If you have a creative streak and can write stories, consider offering to write content for children's books. With increasing demand for reading materials, it's a growing opportunity for writers.

19. Offer Scriptwriting Services for Radio: Radio content remains significant, and you can offer your services to write scripts for radio ad placements or even collaborate on radio shows.

20. Write for Captioning Services: As more video content becomes available online, there is a need for well-written captions to manage audience accessibility. You can develop and market captioning services to expand your skillset and cater to a growing demand.

As you can see, the possibilities are endless in the field of freelance writing. You can leverage your skills and talents to carve out a unique space in the market, which will open new opportunities for diversifying your income streams. By taking advantage of one or more of these opportunities, you can build a sustainable income portfolio and enjoy financial stability in your freelance writing career

Conclusion

Diversifying your income streams is essential to financial success as a freelance writer. By finding multiple sources of revenue, you can increase your earning potential, insulate yourself against sudden changes in the market, and enjoy more opportunities to pursue your passions.

We have explored several strategies for diversifying your income as a freelance writer. These include leveraging your existing talents and opportunities, exploring new markets and niches, and expanding your skill sets. We've also seen specific ideas that you can implement to generate more income, from offering social media management services to writing for children's books and more.

- Diversifying your income streams is crucial for long-term financial success and stability.
- Leveraging your existing talents and opportunities is a great way to create multiple revenue streams
- Exploring new markets and niches can help you uncover new opportunities to increase your earnings.
- Expanding your skill set can lead to more high-paying assignments and increased earning potential.

With these takeaways in mind, you can take the next steps in diversifying your income and creating a more fulfilling and financially rewarding career as a freelance writer.

Chapter 15 Why Freelance Writers Need Systems to Earn a Six-Figure Income

As a freelance writer myself, I know firsthand how overwhelming it can be to manage all aspects of a writing business alone. However, creating systems and processes is essential if you're serious about making a full-time income as a writer.

When I started out, I quickly learned that I needed to have systems in place to ensure my business ran smoothly. Managing everything from marketing to accounting to tax reporting on my own was simply too much to handle without a proper plan in place. That's why I dedicated time and effort to creating 20 systems and processes that would help me succeed as a freelance writer.

In this chapter, I'll share with you the exact systems and processes I use to manage my writing business efficiently. By implementing these systems, you'll free up more time to focus on writing and growing your business. You'll also have more control over your income and be better equipped to earn six-figures as a freelance writer.

1. Marketing Strategies

As a freelance writer, you must proactively market your business year after year. Developing strong marketing strategies will help you reach new potential customers and keep existing clients interested in your services. From developing relationships with industry influencers to creating compelling content that resonates with your target audience, there are various ways to market yourself as a copywriter and ensure long-term success:

- Relationship building - Networking and relationships with industry leaders are key to growing any freelance writing

business. Reach out to bloggers, journalists, editors and other influencers who can provide valuable advice, leads or job opportunities. Also, connect with social media platforms like Twitter, LinkedIn and Instagram.
- Content creation - Creating content that resonates with your target audience is one of the best ways to market yourself as a freelance writer. Develop blog posts, e-books, white papers, infographics and other types of content to help you establish yourself as an expert in your field.
- SEO optimization - Optimizing your website for search engines is essential to attract more potential clients online. Make sure all of your content is properly optimized using keywords related to your industry and ensure any links back to your website are relevant and authoritative.

Once you've established solid marketing strategies, it's time to shift your focus to acquiring new clients. To help you do this, here are some effective strategies you can use to attract more high-quality clients that are a good fit for your business:

- Cold outreach - Reach out to potential clients directly via email or social media platforms with a personalized message highlighting your experience and skills.
- Networking events - Attend networking events in your local area to meet potential customers. Making connections in person often yields better results than online methods.
- Referrals - Ask existing clients for referrals and introductions whenever possible. Word-of-mouth advertising is one of the most effective ways to find new clients.
- Freelance job boards - Check out freelance job boards or websites like Upwork, Fiverr and Guru for potential gigs. Not all of these will be high quality, but it's worth a shot to see if you can find any clients needing your services.

2. Accounting Systems

Bookkeeping and accounting can seem like overwhelming tasks, but they are necessary 'evils' you need to be familiar with. While it may be challenging to keep track of incoming payments and expenses without the help of an accountant, learning some basic strategies for accounting and record-keeping will save you time, stress, and money in the long run. Understanding cash vs. accrual basis accounting and setting up best practices for recording income and expenses is essential to keeping your freelance writing business organized. Additionally, numerous software programs are available that can simplify the process even further. This section will provide an overview of accounting system strategies for freelance copywriters so you can start on the right foot.

Cash Accounting vs. Accrual Basis Accounting

When it comes to tracking finances, there are two basic systems of accounting: cash basis and accrual basis. Cash basis accounting records income when it is received and expenses when paid, so income and expenses appear in the same period. Accrual basis accounting records income when it is earned and expenses when they are incurred – regardless of when the money is actually exchanged between parties.

For freelance copywriters who don't have to keep detailed inventory records, cash-basis accounting may be a simpler option than accrual basis; but for those with large or complex projects that span several months or even years, using an accrual system can give you a better idea of your financial standing at any given moment. It's always a good idea to speak with a CPA or tax professional if you have any doubts about which system is right for you and your business.

Recording Income and Expenses

Regardless of the type of accounting system you choose, it is important to set up best practices for recording income and expenses. Start by setting up an organized filing system to store copies of invoices, bills, and other financial documents. Make sure you track all income sources, including client payments and miscellaneous payments from different platforms or websites. When recording expenses, create a spreadsheet that lists each expense type: office supplies, travel costs, advertising fees, etc. so that you can easily view how much money is being spent in each category. Keep all your receipts together in one place for easy reference when needed.

Financial Reports

Accurate financial records will make generating financial statements and reports easier. These documents will provide an up-to-date view of your income, expenses, and overall profitability. The most common financial reports freelance copywriters use are Profit & Loss (P&L) Statements, Balance Sheets, Cash Flow Statements, Accounts Receivable/Payable Reports, and Bank Reconciliation Reports.

Software Available To Help With Bookkeeping

Several software programs are available to automate the bookkeeping process to make the process even easier for freelance writers. From cloud-based accounting systems such as FreshBooks or QuickBooks Online to specialized invoicing apps like Invoice2Go or Wave Accounting, finding a solution that works best for your business is easy. With the right software, you can track income and expenses, create invoices and financial statements, reconcile bank accounts, and much more – all from one convenient interface.

By understanding different accounting systems and setting up a system for recording income and expenses, freelance copywriters can easily organize their finances. Using specialized software can simplify the process even further – so it is worth exploring some available options to help manage your bookkeeping needs. With some basic knowledge and a few helpful tools, freelance writing businesses will have no trouble staying on top of their finances.

3. Tax Reporting Requirements

It may go without saying that it's important to understand your tax reporting requirements. When you work for yourself and there is no employer withholding taxes from your paycheck, it is up to you to pay the taxes you owe. If you're located in the US, this includes federal income taxes, self-employment taxes, and any applicable state or local taxes.

When paying your taxes as a freelancer, one of the best practices is keeping meticulous records throughout the year. Make sure you keep track of all income and expenses - this will help when filing your return at the end of the year. Additionally, familiarize yourself with estimated quarterly payments that may need to be made during the year to avoid underpayment penalties come April 15th.

The most common forms a freelance writer must complete when filing taxes are the 1040, Schedule C and the Self-Employment Tax form. Additionally, other tax forms may need to be completed if you've earned any income from investments or rental properties.

Consider consulting with a tax professional to ensure that all of your tax reporting requirements have been met correctly. This will provide you with peace of mind knowing that you have taken all the necessary steps for properly filing your taxes as a freelancer.

You can also get helpful advice and guidance on successfully managing taxation issues associated with freelancing by attending workshops and seminars specifically designed for entrepreneurs. These courses offer valuable advice and strategies for properly managing your taxes as a freelancer.

By taking all necessary steps and exercising due diligence when filing taxes, you can better ensure you are correctly meeting their tax reporting requirements. This will help prevent potential penalties or fees for not properly reporting income, expenses and other applicable taxes. With the right information and guidance, filing taxes as a freelance writer can be relatively easy and stress-free.

4. Retirement Savings Strategies

Retirement savings are something that every freelancer should think about, and there are many different options to choose from. That said, it's important to do your due diligence and plan ahead to save enough for retirement or a rainy day. Luckily, there are several strategies that you can use as a freelance writer to prepare for the future. From traditional investments such as stocks and bonds in a SEP IRA to non-traditional investments like Bitcoin and fractional real estate investing, plenty of options are available when it comes to retirement savings. Additionally, it is always best practice to diversify your retirement savings so you don't have all your eggs in one basket. With the right planning and strategies in place, you can create a retirement savings portfolio that suits your needs.

Traditional investments like stocks and bonds are great options for freelance writers looking to save for retirement. SEP IRAs, or Simplified Employee Pension Individual Retirement Accounts, are popular choices among freelancers as they allow maximum contributions based on a freelancer's gross reported income, which can be invested in various stock and bond portfolios.

For those who want to explore more non-traditional investment options, Bitcoin and fractional real estate investing may be something to look into. Bitcoin is a digitally mined cryptocurrency that has gained popularity over the past decade due to its decentralized nature and potential for growth. Fractional real estate investing allows individuals to purchase shares in rental properties without purchasing the entire property.

Regardless of your chosen strategy, it's important to remember the importance of diversifying your retirement savings portfolio. This will help reduce risk and ensure that you have multiple streams of income to fund your retirement. Additionally, it is always best practice to save a portion of your freelance earnings for retirement and rainy day funds to be prepared for any unexpected circumstances.

These are just some strategies that can be used by freelance writers when saving for retirement or a rainy day. The key is to research, devise a plan that works for you, and stick to it! With proper planning and preparation, you can create an effective retirement savings portfolio tailored to meet your goals.

5. Automating Processes

Automation strategies for freelancers include using tools to streamline workflows, scheduling out tasks and communicating with clients, and leveraging software that automates complex tasks. Automation has many benefits for freelance writers, from improved accuracy to better organization of projects.

Automating processes can make managing your freelance writing business more efficient by helping you set up systems and routines that streamline the workflow. Automated task management tools such as Asana or Trello can help you organize projects, so you know exactly what needs to be done at each step of the process. Scheduling out emails and other communications is also an effective strategy for staying on track and ensuring deadlines are met.

Another effective automation strategy for freelance writers is leveraging software that simplifies complex tasks, from bookkeeping and invoicing to tracking time spent on each project. This type of automation takes the manual work out of running a business so that you can focus more energy on your writing.

Common processes in a freelance writing business that could be automated include billing clients quickly and reliably, creating contracts and other paperwork, researching topics, tracking expenses, marketing yourself as a writer, and collecting feedback from clients. Automating these processes will help you save time and ensure accuracy in all business operations.

Hiring a virtual assistant (VA) is another excellent way to optimize your time and resources if you're a freelance writer. A VA can manage the numerous jobs that would otherwise rob you of precious hours, such as researching topics for articles, tracking expenses or creating contracts. They are also instrumental in promoting your services and promptly collecting customer feedback. All this enables you to be more productive while dedicating maximum energy towards what gives you real joy - writing and creating outstanding content!

Hiring a VA can also help save money by allowing you to scale your operations without hiring additional staff or increasing overhead costs. As your business grows, so does the need for experienced professionals who can be trusted to handle certain tasks swiftly and accurately. They can be hired as needed, meaning you pay only for the services you require and can scale up or down depending on your needs.

6. Time Management Strategies

An effective time management strategy will help ensure that you hit your deadlines and produce high-quality work that meets your clients' needs. To give yourself the best chance at success as a freelancer, here are some strategies you can use to manage your time more effectively and grow your business:

- Set realistic goals and break them into manageable chunks – setting achievable goals helps keep you motivated and productive. Break big tasks into smaller pieces, so they don't seem overwhelming or unachievable.
- Schedule regular breaks throughout the day – taking regular breaks helps reduce fatigue and stress, which can positively impact your productivity.
- Prioritize tasks and start with the most important ones – by prioritizing, you can focus on your most important goals first and prevent yourself from getting overwhelmed.
- Track your progress – tracking your progress helps you stay organized, motivated, and focused on completing tasks promptly.
- Learn to say "no" – don't take on too much work or stretch yourself too thin; focus on quality rather than quantity when taking on new jobs or projects.
- Keep distractions to a minimum – limit distractions such as social media, emails, and other interruptions while working so you can remain productive and efficient with your time management.
- Re-evaluate your schedule regularly – as your business grows and changes, re-evaluate your schedule so you can adjust to any new demands or challenges.

By following these strategies and developing an effective time management system that works for you, you'll be better able to increase your productivity and grow your freelance writing business.

7. Outsourcing Tasks

As a freelance writer, you have the ability to manage your own time and workload. However, there may come a time when taking on too much work can become overwhelming and reduce the quality of your writing. Fortunately, outsourcing certain tasks can help lighten that load, allowing you to focus more on the writing itself. Doing so can increase efficiency while freeing up more time for yourself.

Some common tasks that a freelancer might outsource include research, editing, bookkeeping, graphic design and administrative tasks such as email management or scheduling appointments. All of these tasks require specialized knowledge or skills that may not be worth investing in if they are only used once in a while. In addition, delegating these tasks to someone else allows you to focus on the more important aspects of your business, such as marketing and writing.

Outsourcing can also be beneficial from a financial perspective, as it helps minimize overhead costs by reducing the need for full-time employees. By outsourcing specific tasks and services, freelancers can also benefit from economies of scale, meaning they can pay only for the hours that have been worked rather than an entire salary. This allows them to operate more efficiently and save money in the long run.

8. Establishing a Business Entity

Starting your own freelance writing business can be an exciting and rewarding endeavor. But it is important to consider which legal structure best fits the needs of your business. Depending on the size and scope of your freelance writing business, you may need to establish a formal business entity to protect yourself from liability and optimize taxation benefits. Various types of business structures are available, each with advantages and disadvantages. In this section, we'll discuss the various types of entities you can choose for your freelance writing business and their associated pros and cons so that you can make an informed decision about what works best for you.

The most common forms of business entities include sole proprietorships, partnerships, limited partnerships, limited liability companies (LLCs), and corporations. Each entity offers different benefits, so it is important to understand the implications of each type before making a decision.

A sole proprietorship is an unincorporated business owned by one person. It may be the simplest and most affordable form of business structure. Setting up a sole proprietorship typically requires few formalities other than filing the necessary paperwork with local authorities. However, some risks are also associated with this form. The owner of a sole proprietorship is personally responsible for any debts or liabilities incurred by the business, and there is no legal distinction between their personal finances and that of the business.

Partnerships are similar to sole proprietorships in that they are also unincorporated business entities. Generally, partnerships involve two or more individuals working together to run a business. Partnerships are often seen as advantageous because of the shared responsibility among members and the ability to pool resources for a greater potential return. However, similar to sole proprietorships, all partners involved in a partnership have personal liability for any debts or legal issues that may arise from it.

Limited partnerships (LPs) are another form of business entity; however, they involve one general partner who is personally responsible for all debts and liabilities associated with the business and several limited partners with financial stakes but no responsibility for managing the business itself. This structure is useful when multiple investors are involved in a venture as it can help protect against personal liabilities.

Limited liability companies (LLCs) are a popular business entity, offering owners protection from personal liabilities and tax benefits. LLCs are also simpler to set up than corporations, although it is important to note that setting one up does require some paperwork. Additionally, LLCs may or may not be taxed as separate entities depending on the state in which they are formed. This should be considered when deciding which structure best suits your needs.

Finally, corporations are the most complex type of business entity. Corporations can be publicly traded or privately owned and must adhere to more stringent regulations than other entities. While forming a corporation can provide certain advantages, such as greater access to financing and lower taxes, it also involves a great deal of paperwork and is typically more expensive to set up than other business structures.

No matter which entity you choose for your freelance writing business, it is important to carefully consider all of the options available to find the one that best fits the needs of your business. Each entity offers different benefits and drawbacks, so taking the time to research them and speaking with a qualified financial or legal advisor may help you decide what type of business structure works best for you.

9. Building an Online Presence

Having a strong online presence will help you attract new clients and increase visibility in the writing world. It can also help you showcase your skills, build trust with potential customers, and set yourself apart from other freelancers.

The best way for freelance writers to build an online presence is to start with their own website. This is where potential clients can learn more about you, view samples of your work, or contact you for services. When building your website, make sure to include relevant keywords that focus on the type of writing or content creation services you specialize in; this will help boost the site ranking in search engines. It's also important to ensure your website is mobile-friendly, as more and more people are using their phones to browse the web.

Another effective way for freelance writers to build an online presence is through social media. Platforms such as Twitter and LinkedIn are great tools for connecting with other professionals in the writing industry or clients who may be looking for services like yours. You can use these platforms to spread brand awareness, share useful resources related to your field, or even showcase samples of your work. Just remember to keep the content engaging and relevant to drive traffic back to your website.

Finally, email marketing can be a powerful tool for freelance writers to build an online presence. Having an email list allows you to stay in touch with current and potential clients and share updates about services or new projects. You can also use this platform to offer special discounts or promotions that give readers a reason to come back and visit your website.

10. Protecting Your Intellectual Property Rights

You already know that the words and ideas you create are valuable assets. Your work is your intellectual property – and protecting your intellectual property rights should be an essential part of your business strategy. Intellectual property refers to creations of the mind, such as literary works, inventions, symbols, names and images. It is important for freelancers to understand their intellectual property rights and how they can be safeguarded from misuse or infringement by others.

One way to protect your intellectual property is through copyright registration. Registering a copyright provides legal evidence that you own the material, enabling you to pursue legal action against those who violate it. In addition, make sure you always use contracts when working with clients or collaborators so that everyone understands who owns the rights to any created material.

Finally, consider trademarking your writings and other creative works. This way, no one else can use your ideas or writings without permission or credit. With these measures in place, you can ensure that your intellectual property is protected and that you benefit from the fruits of your hard work as a freelance writer.

To learn more about protecting your intellectual property rights, freelancers may want to review the following resources:

1. The United States Copyright Office website provides information on copyright registration and enforcement.

2. The World Intellectual Property Organization (WIPO) for advice on international IP protection laws and regulations.

3. The Small Business Administration's online guide to trademarking for helpful information and tips.

4. Local business law firms specializing in intellectual property law for expert guidance.

5. Professional organizations such as the Writers Guild of America or the National Association of Independent Writers and Editors which offer information, seminars, and workshops on IP-related topics. With

these resources at hand, you can confidently protect your valuable creations and secure your intellectual property rights.

11. Setting Goals and Objectives

Setting goals and objectives as a freelance writer is essential for driving toward success. It provides clarity of purpose, allows you to track your progress, and allows you to evaluate your strategies' effectiveness. When setting goals and objectives, it's important to think realistically about what you can achieve with the resources available to keep yourself motivated.

When creating goals and objectives, make sure they are SMART:

- Specific
- Measurable
- Achievable
- Realistic
- Time-bound

This means that each goal should be specific regarding what needs to be accomplished; have an achievable outcome; be realistic based on the resources available; and have a timeline for completion. For example, instead of setting a vague goal of "getting more clients," set a specific goal such as "attracting five new clients by the end of the year." This will provide you with clear direction and allow you to measure your progress.

In addition to setting SMART goals, creating objectives tied to those goals is important. Objectives should be actionable steps that can help you reach your goal. For example, if your goal is "attracting five new clients by the end of the year, " some objectives might include creating a portfolio website, submitting three guest posts per month, or attending one in-person networking event each quarter.

Creating measurable goals and objectives can help you stay on track and remain motivated throughout the year. Aside from setting goals and objectives, it's important to take the time to review and reflect on your progress regularly. This can help you identify areas for improvement and adjust your approach as needed. With these best practices in mind, you can stay focused, succeed more, and become a high-performing freelance writer.

12. Creating a Reasonable Workflow Schedule

As a freelance writer, it's important to have an organized and reasonable workflow schedule to ensure that you can complete all of your projects on time. A good workflow schedule will help you stay focused, regularly reach deadlines, and increase productivity.

When creating a reasonable workflow schedule, it is important to think about what days and times are most convenient for you to work based on other commitments such as your day job, family or school. It can be helpful to plan out a week at a time so that you know exactly when and how long each project will take. Additionally, grouping similar tasks together can make the process easier by allowing you to work more efficiently. For example, if you need to write multiple blog posts for different clients, you could group them all together and dedicate a specific day to working on those projects.

Another helpful tip for creating a workflow schedule is to plan out your breaks in advance. This will help you stay focused and manage your time better throughout the day. You may even want to consider setting up a few designated work days where you don't take any breaks to ensure that you can stay productive and get more done in less time.

Finally, it's important to remember that a workflow schedule should be flexible and adapted regularly based on the changes in your workload or commitments. An organized workflow schedule allows you to maximize efficiency, reduce stress, and have plenty of time for other activities. The best way to ensure you stay on track and that all of your work gets done is to create a reasonable workflow schedule that works best for you.

13. Planning for Growth and Expansion

As a freelancer, planning for growth and expansion is essential to building a successful writing business. To do this, consider several strategies that will help you to take your writing career to the next level:

- Specializing or diversifying services: As a freelancer, you can achieve growth and success by specializing your services or diversifying your offerings. Specializing enables you to gain experience in one specific area and become an expert in that field. Conversely, diversifying your services provides you with work across multiple areas, ensuring that when one market slows down, another may be booming.
- Reaching out to new clients and markets: Consider localized advertising campaigns or broader campaigns utilizing social media and search engine optimization techniques to reach out to new clients and markets. Attend conferences, networking events, or seminars related to the freelance industry, where you can meet potential new clients while learning more about your industry.
- Forming strategic partnerships: Collaborating with other professionals such as copyeditors, web designers, or marketing professionals can help free up time and resources for you to focus on creating quality content while expanding your reach.
- Using management tools: Streamline processes and improve client communication by using tools like project management software and customer relationship

management systems to keep track of deadlines, budgets, payment schedules, invoices, and past projects for future reference.
- Investing in yourself: As a freelancer, you should continually invest in yourself by taking courses or attending workshops related to your field to stay ahead of trends and hone your craft. By reviewing your progress regularly, logging your accomplishments and benchmarking future goals, you can set yourself up for long-term success.

By implementing these strategies, you can enjoy both financial and non-financial benefits such as increased revenue, improved credibility, better customer service, and greater work/life balance. As an expert freelancer, strategic planning and action will propel your writing business for future success.

14. Managing Risk In Your Business

As a freelance writer, managing risk in your business is essential to ensure that you and your work remain safe. Potential risks may include financial losses due to lack of payment, damage or theft of equipment, and legal issues stemming from plagiarism or copyright infringement. By following best practices for risk management, you can help protect yourself and your business from these potential risks.

When it comes to financial loss, one of the best practices is to use contracts with clients whenever possible. Having a contract outlines the expectations of both parties and establishes protections if those terms are not met. It also helps clarify ambiguous language that could lead to disputes during the payment process. Additionally, establishing clear guidelines around payment processes can help avoid instances of non-payment.

Another potential risk is the theft or damage of your equipment, such as computers and printers, especially if you work as a digital nomad. To protect yourself from this, it is best to purchase insurance that covers these items in case they are damaged or stolen. Additionally, ensuring regular backups of all important work stored on an external hard drive can help minimize any loss if unexpected events occur.

Finally, plagiarism and copyright infringement can lead to legal issues for freelance writers. Practicing good research habits by citing all sources correctly and double-checking for plagiarism will help reduce the chances of accidental infringement. Consider using a service such as Copyscape to check for accidental plagiarism. Additionally, obtaining proper permissions before using copyrighted material can ensure that your use falls within the boundaries of fair use guidelines.

15. Monitoring Progress and Adjusting Strategies As Needed

As a freelancer, it's essential to set measurable goals and track your progress to ensure that you're moving toward your objectives. Monitoring your progress regularly is an effective way to ensure that your strategy is on track and that you're making progress towards meeting your goals.

Additionally, as a freelancer, it's also important to recognize that things don't always go as planned. External factors such as changes to the industry or clients' needs can impact your business, making it necessary to periodically adjust your business strategy. Regularly reviewing your progress enables you to identify potential problems early on, adjust your strategy accordingly, and keep your business aligned with your goals and vision.

By doing so, you can stay on track to achieve your goals and build a thriving writing business. Here are some tips to follow:

- First, measure performance by setting clear goals and tracking how well you meet them. You should also assess the quality of your work—are clients happy with it? Are deadlines being met? And if possible, look at other metrics, such as pageviews for content published online or word count per project, to gauge success.
- Second, use feedback from clients and peers to adjust strategies to meet goals. Listen to what clients and colleagues have to say about your work, and use their feedback to adjust the direction you take.
- Third, make sure you're taking the time to reflect on progress regularly so that you can adjust as needed. Set aside a few hours each month or quarter for this purpose. Analyze how well you meet your goals, review any complaints or concerns from clients, assess the quality of your writing, and consider any changes in the industry that might affect your work.
- Finally, be open-minded when it comes to adjusting strategies as needed. If something isn't working out as planned or there is an opportunity for improvement, don't be afraid to pivot and try something different.

16. Taking Care of Your Mental Health and Well-Being as an Entrepreneur

You're responsible for every aspect of running your business, from managing your finances to marketing your services and creating content. While this level of control can be empowering, it can also be incredibly stressful and overwhelming. As a result, it's essential that you prioritize your mental health and well-being as an entrepreneur.

Maintaining good mental health can help you to manage stress, stay motivated, and make sound decisions. Neglecting your mental health can lead to burnout, which can ultimately hurt the success of your business. Additionally, as a freelancer, you lack the benefits and social connections that often come with traditional employment, which can exacerbate feelings of isolation and loneliness.

Fortunately, there are several strategies you can follow to manage stress and maintain a healthy work/life balance, including establishing a routine, practicing self-care, and staying connected with others:

- Make time for self-care: Schedule in time each day to do something just for yourself. Whether it's going on a walk or reading a book, self-care is essential to staying mentally healthy.
- Get organized: Take the time to get organized to streamline your workflow and reduce stress levels. Create to-do lists, set deadlines, and break down larger tasks into smaller, more manageable ones.
- Manage your stress: Stress can take a toll on your mental health, so it's important to learn how to manage it effectively. Working out or meditating can help you relax and refocus, while taking breaks during the day will also help keep you productive and in a positive mindset.
- Take regular breaks: Regular breaks throughout the day are essential for staying focused and productive. Get up from your desk, move around and use this time to clear your head and think about something else for a few minutes.
- Network with other entrepreneurs: Networking with other entrepreneurs can be beneficial for sharing ideas, support, advice, and motivation – all of which are important for staying mentally healthy.

By implementing these strategies, you'll be able to look after your mental health and well-being as an entrepreneur while remaining productive and successful. With regular self-care, organization, stress management and networking with other entrepreneurs, you can keep yourself motivated and on track toward achieving your goals.

17. Maintaining Professionalism in Your Business

Maintaining professionalism in your freelance writing business is key to building relationships with clients, delivering quality work and becoming a successful freelancer. Here are some strategies you can follow to ensure you remain professional:

- Respond promptly to all inquiries from clients or potential employers. This shows respect for their time, along with the importance of your work.
- Be reliable and honest about deadlines and commitments. Showing that you keep your word will build trust, which leads to more opportunities down the road.
- Respectfully disagree when appropriate. While disagreements are inevitable, they should always be handled professionally by communicating calmly and clearly without resorting to name-calling or other unprofessional behavior.
- Stand your ground on pricing and don't devalue your work by undercharging. Think of yourself as a professional service provider and price accordingly.
- Stay up-to-date on industry trends, news and important topics related to your writing content. This shows potential employers that you are knowledgeable and can provide quality work.

The consequences of unprofessional behavior include loss of repeat clients, damage to reputation, fines or even legal action (in extreme cases). To avoid this, always be polite and respectful when dealing with clients and employers, no matter the circumstance. Additionally, it's important to remain mindful of copyright laws if you have used images or music for a project — make sure everything is properly credited and cited.

Finally, here are a few examples of ways to maintain professionalism in your freelance writing business:

- Write clear contracts with specific terms, deadlines and payment details that both parties agree to.
- Meet deadlines on time (or earlier if possible).
- Always use proper grammar and punctuation when communicating with clients or employers.
- Provide feedback regularly (if requested) and be open to constructive criticism from employers or clients who may have different opinions than yours on how the project should be done.
- Show appreciation for clients' feedback by thanking them for taking the time to provide it — this will also help build trust and respect between you two.

By following these tips, you will be able to maintain professionalism in your freelance writing business while also gaining the trust of clients and employers. The more professional you are, the more successful your business will be.

18. Developing Connections With Other Writers and Professionals in the Industry

It's easy to feel isolated, since much of your work involves sitting in front of a computer. While it's essential to be self-sufficient and able to work independently, it's equally important to connect with others in the industry. Building relationships with other writers and professionals can help you learn from others' experiences, get feedback on your work, and expand your network.

However, with the right connections in place, you can grow your freelance writing business, expand your reach, and find new insights, support, and inspiration. Here are some strategies you can use:

1. Join professional organizations - Organizations such as The International Association of Business Writers (IABW) provide networking opportunities and resources for freelance writers. Joining one of these organizations will give you access to valuable contacts that could lead to future job prospects.

2. Attend conferences - Conferences are great places to meet people in your field. You can learn about the latest trends, find out what other freelancers are doing, exchange business cards, and start building relationships.

3. Utilize social media - Platforms like Twitter and LinkedIn are great for connecting with people in the industry. You can follow writers, professionals, and organizations to get their updates and insights into the field. You can interact with them directly by commenting on posts or sending a direct message.

4. Look for referrals - Ask your friends, family, co-workers, and colleagues if they know anyone who could help you in the freelance writing world. They may be able to provide referrals or even introduce you to someone looking for a writer.

Some freelancers encourage referrals by paying a fee if the referral results in a paying client. Regarding fees, you must decide if the advantages of paying them outweigh the drawbacks. Paying referral fees can be advantageous as they are a great way to expand your network quickly. However, measuring how much value you receive in return for this arrangement can be difficult. Some may opt not to refer anyone out of fear that their reputation might suffer or because they do not wish to feel obligated toward the recipient of their referrals. Ultimately, whether or not you choose to pay out referral fees should be an individual decision based on what works best for your business goals.

These are just a few strategies freelance writers can use to develop connections with other writers and professionals in their field. By taking advantage of these opportunities, you can increase your network and gain valuable experience that will help propel your career forward.

19. Building a Support Network for Yourself as a Freelancer

A support network is a group of people who provide encouragement and advice in times of need. Having a strong support network can be invaluable for freelancers, providing an extra layer of stability and comfort from having like-minded professionals to turn to when needed. Plus, these contacts are great sources of information about the industry, potential projects and job opportunities.

The importance of having a support network as a freelancer cannot be overstated. It's incredibly helpful to have someone who understands the unique struggles and joys of being self-employed, especially if you feel isolated or overwhelmed by all the responsibilities of working independently. A strong support network can also serve as your sounding board as you brainstorm and problem-solve.

When building a support network, there are two main types: business and personal. Business contacts are people who can help you find work or provide professional advice on how to navigate the freelancing world. These could be past clients, colleagues at events or other professionals in your field. Personal contacts could include family, friends or past coworkers –anyone familiar with the freelance lifestyle and willing to lend an ear when needed.

The best strategy for building a successful support network is to start small and focus on quality over quantity. Start by networking within your profession – attend events, join discussion groups online and look for mentors in the industry. As you expand your business connections, don't forget to reach out to your personal contacts as well. Having people who can provide understanding and empathy is just as important as having professionals who are experts in the field.

No freelancer should have to go it alone -- a strong support network is essential for success. Building one takes time and effort, but the rewards of having a dedicated group of confidants by your side will be more than worth it in the end.

20. Staying Up to Date on Trends, Laws, and Technologies That Impact Your Business

Knowing what's happening in the industry allows you to better prepare for challenges and capitalize on possible opportunities. Additionally, understanding the changing trends and legal requirements can help you maintain an edge over competitors and stay competitive.

So how exactly can you stay informed? Below are some strategies to consider:

- Follow relevant blogs or websites: Many great resources are dedicated to providing updates on the latest news in your industry. Make sure to subscribe to newsletters or RSS feeds of popular sites such as JScottDigital.com, Copy Blogger, ProBlogger, etc., to get timely updates on the latest trends and developments.

- Attend conferences: Attending industry-related conferences is a great way to stay up to date with the latest happenings in your field. You can network, learn from experts, and get valuable insights to apply to your business.

- Connect with other freelancers: Networking is key! Reach out to other freelancers in your space and become part of a community or online forum where you can exchange ideas, discuss challenges and successes, and benefit from each others' experiences.

By following these strategies consistently, you will be well informed about what's happening in the industry and any new laws or regulations that may affect freelance writers. Staying up to date on the latest trends and technologies will be a critical ingredient in helping you succeed as a freelancer.

Final Thoughts On Running A Successful Freelance Writing Business

With the right systems and processes in place, you can keep your freelance writing business running smoothly. The strategies discussed in this chapter will help you successfully manage all aspects of your business and help to ensure its continued growth and success.

Learn how to create systems to help you market yourself, handle accounting tasks and protect your intellectual property rights. Automate processes to save time and build an online presence. Develop connections with others in the industry. Set your goals and objectives, maintain professionalism in your work, and stay up-to-date on business trends.

By creating effective systems and processes for managing all aspects of your freelance writing business, you can enjoy a successful career as a freelancer and become a six-figure earner if you so desire.

Conclusion Secrets of the $100,000 Club: Joining the Elite Rank of High-Earning Writers

Congratulations! You've made it to the end of our comprehensive guide on building a successful freelance writing business. Through the 15 chapters, I've shared with you my knowledge and expertise on how to transition from your day job to a lucrative freelance writing career, choose your writing niche, find high-paying clients, negotiate better rates, and diversify your income streams.

Throughout the guide, you've learned how to manage your time effectively, handle rejection, maintain a healthy work/life balance, and prioritize your mental health and well-being as an entrepreneur.

I've shared with you expert strategies for networking, building connections in the freelance writing industry, establishing systems to help you earn a six-figure income, and planning for growth and expansion for your writing career.

Building a successful freelance writing business takes time and dedication, but with the knowledge you've gained from this guide, you'll be able to navigate even the toughest challenges of the freelance writing industry.

Subscribe to Our Weekly Premium Newsletter

As a freelance writer, you need to stay up-to-date with the latest trends and insights in the industry. That's why I'm inviting you to subscribe to our weekly premium newsletter.

As a premium subscriber, you'll get access to exclusive content, insider tips, and resources that will help you stay ahead of the competition and achieve your freelance writing goals.

Don't miss this opportunity to take your freelance writing career to the next level. Subscribe to our weekly premium newsletter today by visiting https://jscottdigital.com/premium-newsletter/

About the Author

Jeff Rohde is an accomplished freelance writer and copywriter who regularly earns six figures per year from his craft. With over a decade of experience in the industry, Jeff has worked with clients across a diverse range of fields, including real estate, finance, investment, insurance, and accounting.

Jeff's professional writing career began with a successful blog about real estate investing, which caught the attention of major clients and led to regular contributions to financial websites. As his reputation grew, Jeff expanded his client base and continued to hone his skills as a versatile and expert wordsmith.

In "$100,000 per Year as a Freelance Writer: It's Possible, and Here's How," Jeff draws on his extensive experience to share practical insights and valuable tips that aspiring writers will find beneficial. He emphasizes the importance of building a personal brand, marketing oneself effectively, and fostering strong relationships with clients.

Jeff's portfolio is a testament to his expertise and versatility as a writer. He has tackled complex topics such as real estate investing, retirement planning, and accounting principles, and has crafted engaging copy for a variety of audiences. From blog posts and editorials to sales copy and white papers, Jeff has consistently provided high-quality content that resonates with readers and delivers results for his clients.

If you're looking to take your writing career to the next level, Jeff Rohde is a trusted advisor who can help you achieve your goals. He is among the top 3% of performers on Upwork and has been awarded the Top Rated Plus badge. Visit his website today to request his services and learn more about how he can help you reach your earning potential as a freelance writer: https://jscottdigital.com/

www.ingramcontent.com/pod-product-compliance
Ingram Content Group UK Ltd.
Pitfield, Milton Keynes, MK11 3LW, UK
UKHW022214230426
12048UKWH00016BA/840